Teenagers:
Why Do They Do That?

'If there's one book I advise parents to read to understand their teenagers, it's this one because it has helped me so much to understand mine.'

Dr Trevor Stammers, Senior Tutor in General Practice at St George's Hospital Medical School, writer and broadcaster

'The cultural world of teenagers is a closed book to many adults. Parents, relatives, neighbours and other onlookers fail to make sense of young people who seem to inhabit a different world from the one in which they live. Nick Pollard has for many years worked with teenagers in contexts where he has encouraged them to reflect upon their own values, beliefs, and behaviour patterns. This provocative book takes the reader into that world in a way which many will find enlightening and helpful.'

Professor Roger Murphy, University of Nottingham

'This is the perfect book to help you understand and communicate with today's youngsters. It is profound, realistic, memorable and, in the end, optimistic. I have read and re-read it, and it has changed the way I talk with both young people and parents.'

Michael Cuthbertson, former Headmaster of Monkton Combe School

To the 6,000 or more teenagers who attend my school conferences each year and discuss their beliefs and values with me so openly and honestly. I hope that I may help you explore spiritual and moral issues. You certainly help me to gain some insight into the impact of modern culture in your lives.

*For information on these school conferences (and to watch a video about them) see **www.damaris.org/schools***

Teenagers:
Why Do They Do That?

Nick Pollard

DAMARIS
www.DamarisBooks.com   **Authentic**

10 09 08 07 06   7 6 5 4 3 2 1

First published in 1998 by Lion Publishing. This revised edition
published in 2006 by Damaris Books, an imprint of
Authentic Media, 9 Holdom Avenue, Bletchley, Milton Keynes,
Bucks, MK1 1QR, UK and 129 Mobilization Drive, Waynesboro,
GA 30830-4575, USA.

Authentic Media is a division of Send the Light Ltd., a company
limited by guarantee (registered charity no. 270162).

British Library Cataloguing in Publication Data
A catalogue record for this book is available
from the British Library.

1-904753-13-2

Cover design by fourninezero design.
Print management by Adare Carwin
Typeset by Textype in Palatino
Printed in the UK by J.H. Haynes & Co., Sparkford

Contents

Introduction

*Two teenage boys brutally beat an 80-year-old
blind man and leave him for dead as they run off
with his pension.*

*A 13-year-old girl is expelled from school for
her abusive behaviour and complete lack of
respect for any authority.*

*An 18-year-old boy, known to be a regular
user of ecstasy, is discovered unconscious in the
toilets of a nightclub, and dies on the way to
hospital.*

*A 17-year-old girl suffocates herself with a
plastic bag, leaving a note to say that she cannot
face taking her exams.*

Almost every day the newspapers report yet more
tragedies that teenagers have inflicted upon themselves
or upon other people. For many of us these are not just
abstract stories in the press. We see similar disasters just
waiting to happen in the lives of our own children, or
those of friends, or those we teach. Every time we hear of
a young person who has started sniffing glue, or taken to

the streets, or become anorexic, many of us ask the same question: 'Why do they do that?'

Why do they criticise everything? Why do they take drugs? Why don't they respect authority? Why do they develop eating disorders? Why are they obsessed with fitting an image? Why are they so sexually promiscuous? Why don't they see the value of old people? Why don't they get up and do something useful? Why? Why? Why?

For many of us, teenagers can be a real mystery. It's as if they have come from another planet. Parents, in particular, can find it very hard to understand them, let alone be held responsible for their actions. We may be tempted to take the advice of Mark Twain, who, it is said, recommended that when a boy gets to thirteen years old he should be sealed in a barrel with just a small hole for air. And then when he gets to fifteen years old the hole should be bunged up.

Through my work with teenagers over the past eighteen years, I have met many parents who feel that they have failed. They have often come to me in tears asking, 'What have I done wrong?' They describe the behaviour of their son or daughter, and then say, 'It must be our fault.' This book is written for all those parents who feel like this. I hope that, after reading it, you will find those feelings of guilt and failure will lift from your shoulders.

Of course there are things that parents can do to relate better to their teenage children and to help them more effectively. We will look at some of these in Chapter 7. But, before we can consider how we might respond to any particular teenage behaviour in any particular situation, we must obtain a general understanding of why it is that so many teenagers behave in the way they do. We can't think about particular solutions until we have understood the underlying causes. So each of the first six chapters of this book will look at a different feature of some teenage behaviour and examine the fundamental causes that lie behind it.

We will then see that many of these root causes lie not so much in the home, or in the parents, but rather in the massive shifts that have taken place in Western culture in recent years. This, then, is not a book about parenting teenagers so much as a book about understanding the culture in which teenagers live. But I have no doubt that as you begin to understand this culture better you will be able to understand your particular teenagers better, and then be able to help them more effectively.

Things Aren't What They Used to Be

The term 'teenager' was coined, in 1942, by market researchers who were looking for a new category of young people to whom they could target their goods. Since then a lot has changed.

At that time, if you asked a teenage boy what he most wanted he would probably tell you that most of all he wanted 'a suit just like my dad's'. Today, that's the very last thing he wants!

According to the California Police Department and the Department of Education in Fullerton, California, the top seven discipline problems in schools in 1940 were: talking in class, chewing gum, getting out of line, running in the halls, making a noise, wearing improper clothes and not putting waste in the waste-paper basket. However, in 1990 the top seven problems had become: drug abuse, alcohol abuse, pregnancy, rape, suicide, robbery and assault.

There is no doubt that teenagers are very different today. And so is the world in which they live. Our culture has gone through massive changes in the last few decades – at a depth, a scale and a pace that have never before been known in the history of civilisation. Unless we are aware of these changes and have thought through their implications, we will not be able to understand the teenagers who are growing up among them. Nor will we even begin to have any answer to that constant question: 'Why do they do that?'

Douglas Rushkoff, the American journalist and social commentator, has observed 'Our world is changing so rapidly that we can hardly track the differences, much less cope with them. Whether it's call-waiting, MTV, digital cash, or fuzzy logic, we are bombarded every day with an increasing number of words, devices, ideas and events that we do not understand. On a large-scale, the cultural institutions on which we have grown dependent – organised religion, our leaders and heroes, the medical establishment, corporate employers, even nation states and the family itself – appear to have crumbled under their own weight, and all within the same few decades. Without having migrated an inch we have nonetheless travelled further than any generation in history.'[1]

We must wake up to the fact that we are in uncharted waters. Never before, in the history of civilisation, has a generation grown up amongst such extensive cultural change. During the last few decades almost all of Western culture's underlying beliefs and values have been turned upside down. Philosophically, we have shifted from modernism to post-modernism (don't worry, this will all be explained later!). Educationally, we have moved from a didactic to a critical teaching model (and this!). Sociologically, many of our communities and families have disintegrated. Psychologically, new ways of viewing brain function have destroyed the previously foundational concepts of our individual identity. Politically, the fall of communism has rewritten the world map. Economically, the triumph of individual consumerism over socialism has changed the way in which we determine value. Medically, previously impossible treatments have become commonplace and expected. Technologically, computers and the Internet have offered us instant access to information throughout the world. And so the list goes on.

Wherever we look in Western culture there have been massive changes during the last few decades. Should we be surprised, then, when those of us who grew up before those changes took hold find it hard to understand those who are growing up knowing only a world full of such changes?

Clearly it is inevitable that we should be puzzled by teenage behaviour. They are so different to the way we were at their age, because the world in which they are growing up is so different from the world we knew, even as little as twenty or thirty years ago.

And yet this is the world that we all know today. There are certain aspects of teenage culture which are unique to teenagers. But much of teenage culture is shared with the wider culture in which we all live. Indeed, most of the influential cultural changes we will consider in this book are general cultural changes not just limited to teenage subculture. Here, then, lies a curious paradox. We find it hard to understand teenagers because we don't understand the world in which they are growing up – and yet that world is the same world in which we ourselves live right now. It is not the world in which we grew up. It is not the world that shaped us through our formative teenage years. But it is the world in which we live today. So why, then, don't we understand it?

Perhaps the answer to that paradox lies in an old Chinese proverb which says, 'If you want to know what water is like, don't ask a fish.' The more we are surrounded by something, the less we are aware of it. We can become so familiar with things around us that we don't really think about them at all. When I travel in America people sometimes say to me, 'Gee, I love your accent.' That always takes me by surprise, because I don't think that I have an accent. They are the ones who have the accent. I just talk normally. But of course I do have an accent, only I am so used to it that I am not even aware of it.

In the same way, although we live in this world, many of us do not have a clear insight into it. In any case, most of us are so busy surviving that we don't have the time to reflect upon the underlying nature of our culture. But we must do so. We must become aware of our social and philosophical 'accents', because it is only when we understand our world at this deeper level that we will be able to respond to the issues we face on the surface.

I hope that, as you read this book you will be able to take time to think about the world in which we live, in particular to consider the effect that the massive cultural changes of the last few decades have had upon today's teenagers. Only when we understand why teenagers behave in the way they do will we be able to think clearly about how things might be different. Although we may not be individually responsible for the shifts that have taken place in our world, perhaps together we can do something about them.

That is why Chapter 7 contains not only suggestions as to what we might do on an individual and family basis, but also things we might call for in society at large. If our changed culture is having such a devastating effect upon today's teenagers, then, for the sake of tomorrow's teenagers, we must see our culture change again – not necessarily back to how it was, but perhaps onwards to something far better.

Some of the underlying concepts examined in the chapters ahead will take some effort to understand. They are not all easy – but they are all vital. It is always less difficult to look at just the surface of things, but that is not usually where the real answers are to be found. Indeed, simple, superficial answers can mislead us terribly.

The writer and commentator Os Guinness used to tell a story about a security guard at a Russian factory. One day this guard stopped a worker, who was walking out of the factory gate, pushing a wheelbarrow with a suspicious-looking package in it. The guard opened up the package to find that it contained nothing but some old bits of rubbish, sawdust and sweepings from the floor. The next day he stopped the same worker, who was again pushing a wheelbarrow containing a suspicious-looking package. Once more it contained nothing of value. After the same thing had happened many days in succession the guard finally said to the worker, 'Okay, I give up. I know you must be up to something, but I don't know what it is. I promise I won't arrest you. But please put me out of my misery. Tell me what you are stealing.' The worker looked at the guard and smiled as he replied, 'Wheel-barrows, my friend. I'm stealing wheelbarrows.'

Rather like that guard, we can spend our time looking at the surface of things and miss the real answers that might be found if only we would look and think deeply enough. So let's try to get below the surface. Let's probe into our culture and try to analyze it. Let's be prepared to look back in history. Let's be willing to think about underlying philosophies. Let's do whatever it takes, in order to answer the question, 'Why do they do that?'

Notes

[1] D. Rushkoff, *Children of Chaos (Surviving the End of the World as We Know it)*, HarperCollins, 1997.

Chapter 1

All You Ever Do is Criticise

You can always tell a teenager . . .
but you can't tell him much
(A CAR WINDOW STICKER)

Employ a teenager . . .
while he still knows everything
(ANOTHER CAR WINDOW STICKER)

'I'm at the end of my tether,' Cathy[1] said as she came into my room. 'Why do my kids have to be so critical all the time? They simply won't accept anything I say. They have always got to question it and criticise it. They used to be so nice and easygoing. But since they became teenagers they have turned into a bunch of cynics.'

Cathy has three teenage children. They are all getting on well at school. They do their fair share of messing around and they usually leave their homework to the last minute but they work hard when they have to, they pass their exams and they have a good group of friends. They are not a difficult or disruptive minority. In fact, they are very average teenagers. And, like many teenagers, they

1

do have a tendency to criticise everything and they have become cynical about many things.

Cathy is an intelligent woman, a former teacher. But she clearly had no idea why her children had become so critical. She thought that, in some way, it must be her fault – she must have brought them up badly. When she came to see me she was convinced that, as a parent, she was a dismal failure.

I made Cathy a cup of tea and sat her down in a chair. I then spent the next quarter of an hour explaining to her the educational changes that have taken place in our schools over the past few decades and the philosophical changes that have taken place in the wider culture through the same period. At first she couldn't believe how any of this would help her with the problem she faced with her teenagers. She clearly thought the consultation was going to have as much relevance as learning about the finer points of South Vietnamese glass-blowing.

But then, suddenly, her face lightened. She looked up with a smile. 'Now I see,' she said. 'Of course, I should have realised. I saw these changes begin when I was still teaching. But I didn't realise how much effect they would have upon today's teenagers.'

Cathy had just had what psychologists call an 'aha experience'. This is a situation where people say, 'Aha, now I understand.' For Cathy the light had dawned, the penny had dropped. I hadn't given her a set of quick, superficial tips on parenting teenagers. She didn't need that. But I had helped her to see some of the root causes underlying her teenage children's behaviour. We then were able to spend the next half-hour thinking through specific ways in which she could help them from now on.

Many of us are like Cathy. We look at critical, even cynical, teenagers and ask ourselves, 'Why do they do that?' So let's try to answer that question by considering the underlying causes that I explained to Cathy that afternoon. Let's look at some educational theory and then some philosophy. You might think, as Cathy did at first, that these can't be relevant, but please stick with me, and wait for the 'aha experience'.

A Shift in Education Leads to Criticism

In the world of education, teachers don't just teach in any way they want to. They follow a particular model or theory of education. Over the last few decades a major shift has taken place in the educational model that most schools and colleges use. Most educational establishments have changed from teaching according to the 'didactic model' to using the 'critical method'.

The application of the didactic model in education is sometimes referred to as 'teacher-centred teaching'. This assumes that education is a process through which knowledge that is held by the teacher is passed on to the pupil. When a school follows this model of education, the teacher speaks while the students listen. To facilitate this the classroom is set up with rows of desks at which the pupils all sit still, facing the teacher, listening carefully and taking appropriate notes.

This was the style of education that I experienced throughout my time at school in the 1960s and early 1970s. Whether I was learning History, Physics or Geography, I was taught a body of knowledge by the teachers, which I was then expected to learn and to reproduce in regular tests and examinations.

Through this educational model, I was taught a set of answers and was later given a set of questions. However, a few years later, when I arrived at university, I was given a set of questions for which I had not yet been given the answers. This came as quite a shock to me.

I remember, very clearly, that first week at University. My tutor gave me a book to read and asked me to criticise it. I wasn't quite sure what he expected me to do, so I asked him to clarify his instructions.

'I want you to read this book,' he said, 'and then to tell me where you think the author is right and where you think he is wrong.'

That seemed very strange to me. I wasn't used to this form of education at all. 'But how can I do that?' I asked him. 'The author knows far more about the subject than I do – who am I to criticise him?'

Up until that point of my education I hadn't really learned how to criticise. I knew how to listen carefully, how to learn information, how to organise it in my memory, even how to answer questions that tested my knowledge. But I didn't really know how to criticise.

However, I soon learned. The university taught me how to criticise: books, research results and theoretical papers. And I, quite naturally, transferred that skill outside of my studies. I learned how to criticise politicians, TV programmes, church leaders, other students, parents. In fact I became proficient in criticising anything and everything that dared to move. I was becoming skilled in the critical method.

The application of the critical method in education is sometimes called 'student-centred learning'. This assumes that education is a process through which students explore, question, and formulate truth for themselves. When the teacher follows this model of education, she enables the students to work on their own – investigating, discussing and debating. To facilitate this the classroom should not contain rows of desks but, rather, different areas where students can work on their own or in groups. In this environment the students are encouraged not simply to accept knowledge from other people but to find it out for themselves, to have their own opinions, to make up their own minds.

The philosopher R.S. Peters[2] argued that education must be distinguished from instruction or training, since the goal is for students to develop a 'rational autonomy', the ability to think for themselves and to make their own decisions. That is the aim of the critical method.

The application of the critical method in education is often thought of as a modern development. That isn't strictly true.[3] However, it is only in the last few decades that this method has become widely applied throughout the educational system.

I personally experienced the shift from the didactic model to the critical method when I went to University in 1974. At that time, however, the whole educational system was moving from the didactic to the critical method. While I was at University, and in the years that followed, the grammar school I had left moved from the didactic to the critical method. So did the junior school I had attended. And so did almost every school and college in Britain.

This shift in teaching models, even in the primary schools, was in Britain largely driven by the gradual implementation of the 1967 Plowden report. This was a Government-appointed committee, headed by Lady Plowden, which argued that schools must 'set out deliberately to devise the right environment for children, to allow them to be themselves . . . [it must] lay special stress on individual discovery . . . [so that the child can] look critically at the society of which he forms a part.' This, then, paved the way for the development of new approaches to education throughout our schools and colleges – and, in particular, the adoption of student-centred learning based upon the critical method.

At the same time, since no part of any culture is an island, and all changes in one area tend to affect others, the adoption of the critical method in schools has been mirrored by a shift in other media through which young people are educated, such as TV programmes, magazines, youth groups and churches. In each of these one can see a parallel movement from the didactic model to the critical method.

For instance, increasingly through this period, youth TV programmes didn't just expect viewers to sit and watch. They invited them to interact, to respond, to question and criticise. They asked them to express their own opinion. Similarly, teenage magazines increasingly encouraged their readers to question the traditional beliefs and values of mainstream culture.

Even in churches, which have often been condemned for lagging behind the times, the same shift took place. Over the past few decades many churches started housegroups where church members met to discuss and debate rather than simply to sit in rows listening to the vicar preach. And in church youth groups and Sunday Schools, young people were no longer expected to sit and listen, but were encouraged to question, to criticise, and to express their own views.

In the last few years, there has been pressure to move back towards the didactic model. In Britain, both Labour and Conservative governments, have called for a return to whole-class teaching in the schools. It is possible that the pendulum may swing completely back in that direction in the years ahead. However, no matter what happens in the future, we cannot change the past.

The fact is that today's teenagers have grown up in an educational world, both inside and outside of school, that is based almost wholly upon the critical method. Consequently they tend to be critical. We have taught them how to criticise. And they have become very good at it.

But, if that explains why they may tend to be critical, it doesn't explain why they can also be cynical.

There is clearly a difference between criticism and cynicism. Criticism is a way of seeking out answers. Cynicism is a belief that there are no answers that can be found. Criticism is a methodology. Cynicism is a conclusion. Criticism questions other people's beliefs and values. Cynicism rubbishes them.

In the last few pages, we have discovered one of the major reasons why many teenagers tend to be critical, by looking at some educational theory. Over the next few pages, in order to understand one of the major reasons why teenagers may be cynical, we will have to look at some philosophy.

A Shift in Philosophy Leads to Cynicism

The idea of philosophy may sound a bit boring. I spend a lot of my time teaching philosophy to teenagers and, before they get started most of them assume that it must be about as exciting as tidying their sock drawer. However, they soon realise that philosophy is actually very interesting. Because it is about people. It is all about how people think, why they think in a particular way, why they believe what they believe. People don't do philosophy only in universities. They also do philosophy in the pub, or on the golf course, or over the garden fence.

So we are going to do some philosophy now. We are going to consider what people think about the big questions in life. To do this we have to start by looking back in history.

In the Middle Ages (roughly the fifth to the fourteenth centuries) most people simply thought the way that they were told to think. The church, and others in authority, gave people a set of beliefs that they had to accept. They were not encouraged or even allowed to question this dogma.

Then things began to change. In pubs, over the garden fences and in universities, people began to think differently. A philosophical revolution took place. The stage was set in the fifteenth and sixteenth centuries, the period now known as the Renaissance, which means 'rebirth'. But the change really took off in the seventeenth and eighteenth centuries, a time that became known as the Enlightenment or the Age of Reason.

The Enlightenment began with people such as the Italian astronomer Galileo Galilei (1564–1642), who started to use the newly invented telescope and subsequently rejected the dogma that the earth is at the centre of the Universe. He was ordered to recant, and forced to spend the last eight years of his life under house arrest. Subsequently, other writers, artists and philosophers began to reject other dogmas of the church and placed their hope in the human ability to reason. At this time the German philosopher Immanuel Kant (1724–1804) popularised the catch-phrase 'sapere aude' which means literally 'dare to be wise' – he asked people to risk thinking for themselves. Similarly the French writer Voltaire (1694–1778) called people to be free – to think freely, to act freely.

The Enlightenment ushered in an age of great optimism. People thought that we were going to be able to solve all our problems ourselves. As long as we could think freely and act freely, all would be well. The world was going to get better and better. We could find the answers to life ourselves. We could overcome any obstacle. The culture that was based upon these Enlightenment ideals was called 'modernism'. And this is the world in which we have lived for the past few hundred years.

Modernism placed great faith in the human ability to reason. Rationality was the central idea. Objectivity was sought and prized. As long as we could be set free from the shackles of superstitious church dogma, then we would be able to solve our problems through our ability to reason. For a long time this Enlightenment optimism appeared to be justified. The rationality of modernism saw great advances in science, arts and literature.

However, in recent years, that Enlightenment optimism has faded away. People have begun to realise that the hopes, dreams and promises of modernism have not been fulfilled. We have not been able to solve all our problems. We don't appear to have all the answers. Consequently, the optimism has turned to pessimism.

Thus, Western culture is increasingly rejecting modernism and turning to a new philosophy which is often called 'post-modernism'. This is not really a proper name for the new philosophy, because no one really knows what it is; we just know that it is 'post' (that is, it comes after) modernism.[4]

The term 'post-modern' was first used in 1917, by the German philosopher Pannwitz. It was taken up in literary criticism in the 1950s and 1960s, and then in architecture in the 1970s. The most famous formulation of post-modernism was given in Jean-Francois Lyotard's *The Post-modern Condition*, published in 1979. In this book Lyotard defined postmodernism as 'an incredulity towards meta-narratives'.[5]

According to post-modernism there are no overall answers. There are not really any answers at all – there are only questions. Everything is questioned, even the questions themselves. Whereas modernism led to a world viewed as a community of men and women bound together in a common search for answers, post-modernism is leading to a world of individuals floating in a sea of uncertainty.

Jean Baudrillard, the post-modern Professor of

Sociology at Nanterre said[6] that he saw the world as like a party to which an extraordinary number of people have, alas, failed to turn up – and unfortunately these are the people we knew and thought of most highly. Baudrillard writes of what is not there, what went missing, what is no more, what has lost its substance, ground or foundation. The major trait of our times, he insists, is disappearance. History has stopped. So has progress, if there ever was such a thing. He said that the things we live with today are simply the remnants left over. The world is no longer a scene (a place where the play is staged and directed towards some concrete ending). Instead, it is obscene – a lot of noise and hustle without a plot.

This may sound very academic. One may be tempted to think that post-modernism must only be of relevance to a few isolated, and rather strange, philosophers. However, like it or not, understand it or not, it affects all of us. Our culture has become increasingly post-modern. Let me illustrate this with two examples drawn from everyday culture, one from TV and the other from cinema.

In the world of television there has been a clear move from modern to post-modern programming. The BBC and ITV both offer breakfast TV shows. These are modernistic. We see and hear only the presenters who give us logical, sequential information. They tell news stories. They give us answers to questions. This was true of all British breakfast television until Channel 4 came up with *The Big Breakfast*. This was much more post-modern. We heard not only the presenters, but also the studio crew. The previously secure and reassuring barriers between the roles of presenters and camera operators were broken down. The format was wacky, zany, fast-moving and chaotic. And although the show was cancelled in 2002, it was followed by *Ri:se* – aiming at a similar audience and taking a similar approach. Post-modern television does not seek to tell us much in the way of serious news stories; nor to give coherent answers to the big questions of the day. This is simply life on the surface – more image than substance.

Similarly in the film world we can see a shift from the modern to the post-modern. Douglas Rushkoff[7] has highlighted this transition by comparing the films *Forest Gump* and *Pulp Fiction*. *Forest Gump* is a modernistic film, offering us a sequential, historical journey through the years since World War II. Themes are developed and explored. Messages are communicated. Information is given. *Pulp Fiction* on the other hand is postmodern. This film does not tell a sequential story. Scenes take place in the wrong order. Dead characters reappear. We jump from one time to another. As Douglas Rushkoff describes it, 'Every scene has elements from almost every decade – a 1950s car, a 1970s telephone, a 1940s style suit, a 1990s retrograde nightclub – forcing the audience to give up its attachment to linear history and accept instead a vision of American culture as a compression of a multitude of eras, and those eras themselves being reducible to iconography as simple as a leather jacket or dance step.'

As we can see from these examples, post-modernism leads to chaos. It is born out of pessimism and is maintained by confusion. Therefore it is deeply unsettling. If we are old enough to have grown up in the years before post-modernism took hold, then we have experienced a security, from modernism, which may help us to cope with the post-modern chaos. However, that is not the case for today's teenagers. They are the first generation to have grown up in a world of post-modern confusion. And it clearly has a massive effect upon them.

'What's the point!' said Andy as we chatted together

on the floor of his school common room. His comment was not a question, but a statement. He was not seeking an answer but expressing his pessimistic view of the pointlessness of life. 'It's all rubbish, there's no point,' he continued. I wish I could say that Andy was a very unusual teenager, but his attitude is, unfortunately, typical of many for whom the addition of post-modernism to the critical method has moved them from criticism to cynicism.

Andy had been educated to ask questions, and to seek knowledge by critical enquiry. But, at the same time, he had grown up in an increasingly postmodern culture. Through this he had picked up the idea that there are no satisfactory answers that can be given. There is no reliable knowledge that can be found. Whether or not he had heard it explicitly stated, he had responded to the clarion call of post-modernism: 'We are not seekers after truth – what is the point if there is no truth to find?'[8]

So Andy knew how to ask questions. But he didn't want to listen to any answers, whether they came from me, his parents, or anyone else. And why should we expect him to? For he had clearly absorbed the post-modern idea that there are no satisfactory answers. So why bother looking? He knew how to criticise. He knew how to take things apart. But he didn't seem to be interested in putting things together again. His criticism had become cynicism.

Andy had never heard of post-modernism, nor of the critical model of education for that matter. He had precious little insight into why he thought and acted as he did. He didn't really understand it. He just knew that he wanted to criticise things, and then cynically declare that they were rubbish.

I never met Andy's parents. But I suspect that they were probably puzzled over Andy's attitude and behaviour. Possibly they thought that it was their fault. They may have lain awake at night asking themselves, 'Where did we go wrong?' However, if they had understood the educational and philosophical world in which Andy had grown up, perhaps they would ask a different question: not 'Where did we go wrong?' but rather 'If these really are the underlying reasons for his attitude and behaviour, what then can we do about it?'

We will look at a few answers to that question in Chapter 7. But, before we get there, we have some other features of some teenage behaviour to consider.

Notes

[1] Cathy is not her real name. I will give false names to almost all the people whose stories I tell in this book. This is partly to protect their identity, and partly so that people will still talk to me in the future without fear of being identified in a book! Indeed, some of the individual stories I tell through the book are compilations of a number of different people and situations.

[2] R.S. Peters, *Education and the Education of Teachers*, Routledge, 1977.

[3] In the fifth century BC, the philosopher Socrates taught through asking a series of questions; this is now usually called the 'Socratic method'.

[4] Of course 'post-modernism' is an inadequate name. It is also a misleading one, since post-modernism is not really an '-ism' at all. It isn't a coherent set of beliefs that constitute a complete metanarrative. In fact it is based upon the rejection of coherent sets of beliefs and the abandonment of a search for a complete metanarrative. Therefore it is better described as 'post-modernity' rather than 'post-modernism'.

[5] A 'metanarrative' is an overall way of understanding the world. Marxism is a metanarrative, so are Islam and Christianity, since they each claim to give a complete big story that explains the whole world.

[6] See J. Baudrillard, *Selected Writings*, edited and introduced by M. Poster, Polity Press, 1988.

[7] D. Rushkoff, *Children of Chaos (Surviving the End of the World as We Know it)*, HarperCollins, 1997.

[8] D. Boulton, *Sea of Faith*, No. 16, January 1994.

Chapter 2

Dancing with Death

*38 per cent of 15-year-olds have used illicit
drugs during the past year*
DEPARTMENT OF HEALTH 2003[1]

*. . . drug dabbling is now as normal a part of
growing up as spots.*
CAMBRIDGE UNIVERSITY NEWSPAPER

In November 1995 one picture seemed to dominate the front page of every newspaper in Britain. It showed a pretty teenage girl with a plastic tube strapped into her wide open mouth. Leah Betts had taken a tablet of ecstasy at her eighteenth birthday party. Within a few hours she had collapsed in excruciating agony. At the inquest into her death her father and mother described their desperate attempts to save her. 'She was screaming at the pain in her legs and stomach,' said her father, 'screaming "Mum, please help me."' Her mother recalled how Leah clawed at her for help, before she suddenly fell still and stopped breathing.

Tragically, Leah's death was not an isolated case. Many

other teenagers have died from this drug, and the figures are increasing. During the period 1985 to 1989 eight teenagers died from ecstasy (or similar substances), but by the period 1991 to 1995 the figure had increased to thirty-two.[2] The number of teenagers dying from other drugs, such as heroin, is even greater.

Two months before Leah's death, Elias Fawcett, the 17-year-old son of a senior journalist on *The Economist*, decided to try a drug that would give him the ultimate high. It turned out to be uncut heroin and the next morning he was found dead. Two months after Leah's death, Alexander Balchin, the son of a government education advisor, took a tablet of ecstasy at an all-night rave party and then leapt a hundred feet to his death.

I could go on, listing tragedy after tragedy. If I did so, we would notice how many of the victims seem to have been quite normal, well-adjusted teenagers who apparently had everything going for them. Leah was a happy girl from a loving family. Alexander was described by his father as a fun-loving person who brought joy to the people who knew him. Elias seemed to have everything to live for. He had just completed his A levels, his weekly rave at a Notting Hill club was a success and he was a singer in an emerging rock band.

There was a time when drug abuse seemed to be mainly restricted to a particular subgroup of young people. Other teenagers referred to them as 'druggies' and tended to keep their distance. But this is no longer the case. It is not just those who are rebellious or those from socially disadvantaged families who are using drugs. This activity has become a regular feature of mainstream youth culture.

Recent research surveying over 10,000 pupils from 331 different schools revealed that 38 per cent of 15-year-olds had used illicit drugs over the past year (not including alcohol or tobacco).[3] In the last third of the twentieth century, the use of illegal substances among young people dramatically increased in America to a peak in 1999, when 55 per cent were reported to have used an illicit drug by the time they had left high school. Since then this trend has reduced to a figure of 51 per cent in 2004. However, for the second consecutive year, the lifetime use of inhalants had increased significantly in 8th graders from 15.8 per cent in 2003 to 17.3 per cent in 2004. Unlike the attitude towards ecstasy and marijuana, there is a reported decline in the perceived risk of inhalants since 2001.[4]

A 1996 Government report[5] gave this dreadful conclusion: 'So many young people use or experiment with alcohol and illicit drugs that this behaviour cannot be justifiably described as abnormal'.

Indeed, a UK study published by the Schools Health Education Unit in April 2005, reported that cannabis use in 14–15-year-old boys had increased from 2 per cent in 1987 to 26 per cent in 2004 and 2 per cent to 27 per cent in girls.[6] David Regis, the author of the study explained that these figures are due in part to the increased availability of cannabis. *The Times* predicted that the rise in use of this drug will fuel calls for a change in the legal status of cannabis after it was down graded from class B to class C in 2004.[7] This is of particular concern following medical research reporting that early use of cannabis in a vulnerable minority of young people carries the risk of adults psychological disorders.[8]

Even teenagers who are currently affiliated to churches are using drugs. A 1996 survey[9] conducted by the Evangelical Alliance revealed that 9.7 per cent of the church affiliated 12–16-year-olds questioned had taken drugs at some time. Furthermore the preliminary findings from the National Study of Youth and Religion, a four-year project due to be completed in August 2005, reports that although religiously active teenagers are significantly less likely to engage in risky behaviours, 40 per cent of those who stated that faith was 'very important' in their lives had used illegal drugs in the past year.[10]

Today's teenagers seem to be surrounded by drugs. Research from the Department of Health in 2003, demonstrated that 42 per cent of young people aged between 11 and 15 had been offered drugs, with 61 per cent of 15-year-olds believing that it would be easy to access an illegal substance.[11] A similar American Survey[12] revealed that 68 per cent of 17-year-olds know where they could obtain drugs within a day if they decided to use them. An alarming finding from a follow up survey in 2003, demonstrated that 20 per cent of 12–17-year-olds could obtain marijuana in under an hour.[13]

Should they decide to experiment, they will find that the drugs are not only easily obtainable, but also easily affordable. When ecstasy first hit the dance scene in the 1980s, a tablet cost as much as £25. Today, it can apparently be bought for less than a pound.[14] *The Sunday Times* reported the words of one 17-year-old who explained, 'I could get a tab of LSD for £2.50, or I could get 100 for £30 – just 30p a tab. It was as easy as walking into a shop. I used my pocket money or paper round money . . . I started dealing LSD to pupils of 13 and 14.'

Indeed, drugs are becoming a serious pre-teenage problem. A survey carried out by the Centre for Drug Misuse at the University of Glasgow, revealed that a third of 10–12-year-olds had been exposed to drugs, 1 in 10 had been offered drugs and almost 1 in 20 had started to use them.[15] Professor Neil McKeganey, head of the Centre for Drug Misuse said: 'If we fail to meet the needs of these vulnerable young people we will face the horrifying prospect of increasing numbers of children who have become addicted to illegal drugs before their voices have broken.'[16]

Dying of Ignorance?

When faced with such dreadful statistics, we know that something must be done – but what?

'Education' seems to be the most common answer: we must teach people about the risk of taking drugs. According to this view, if teenagers knew the harm that drugs can do, then they wouldn't take them. This belief is rooted in the ethical philosophy of the Greek thinker Plato,[17] who argued that no one would ever do what is wrong if they knew what is right. If we can teach people the right path, then they will follow it – people only do the wrong thing because of ignorance. Thus, the argument goes, if only we can help teenagers to see that taking drugs is dangerous, then they will 'just say no'.

Consequently, millions of pounds are poured into drug education projects in the UK. Drug information officers have done a great job in warning people of the dangers of drugs. This must be continued. We are not born with such knowledge; we have to learn at some time that drugs are dangerous – and what better way than through a good drug information officer? But is this the complete answer?

Once teenagers are educated properly do they stop taking drugs? Do they just say no? Unfortunately not. In my work with 16 and 17-year-olds, I find that most of them are quite aware of the dangers of drugs. American teenagers between 12 and 17 years have recently reported that 38 per cent of their friends smoke marijuana, an increased of 6 per cent from the previous year.[18] A 2004

UK study reported that up to 61 per cent of 14–15-year-olds are 'fairly sure' or 'certain' that they know a drug user.[19] Many of them personally know individuals who are suffering from their abuse of drugs. According to a 1996 American survey,[20] 43 per cent of 17-year-olds had a friend with a serious drug problem. However, even when they know the dangers, they still take the drugs.

This was most clearly illustrated by the case of Helen Cousins.[21] At a New Year's Eve nightclub party in 1996 Helen took a tablet of ecstasy and sank into a coma. She very nearly died. Before she left hospital she issued a very public warning to all teenagers that drugs were not worth the 'dance of death'. This was carried in newspapers across the country and she was portrayed as a young person who had learned her lesson and would always, from now on, just say no.

However, only a few months later Helen was arrested for being in possession of a tin of amphetamine powder. She and her friends had taken some and then been involved in a car accident. How much more education does she need about the danger of drugs? Is she likely to die of ignorance?

Unfortunately the drug problem will not be solved just by warning teenagers of the dangers. If only the solution were that simple! In fact, if it were that easy, we might have cracked it by now. But we haven't. We must consider a more difficult route. We must take a step back and look much more deeply at the problem. If mere ignorance of the dangers is not an explanation, why is it that teenagers take drugs? What are the root causes underlying this behaviour?

Our first step must be to ask teenagers themselves why it is that they take drugs. I often do that, and I find that they usually give me one or more of three different answers. They tell me that they take drugs to deal with boredom, to join in with their friends, or to cope with the pain in their lives.

In a more structured and formal way, researchers at Columbia University asked 17-year-olds the same question. These teenagers gave a similar response.[22] 22 per cent said that drugs relieve their boredom,[23] 26 per cent said that they took them because of their friends and 23 per cent said that drugs make them feel good. A follow up study by the same research group in 2003, emphasised the increased risk of substance abuse in highly stressed teenagers (twice as likely as low stress teens to smoke, drink, get drunk and use illegal drugs), and in those who often experience boredom (50 per cent more likely to be involved with substance abuse).[24]

So let's look at each of those three reasons and, once again, dig below the surface to see if we can discover some underlying causes. In this chapter, I will look at only the first two. I will deal with the third reason in the next chapter, since the underlying cause that we will discover there leads to other teenage behaviour besides drug-taking, so we will need a whole chapter to think it through.

Dealing with the Boredom

One might wonder how teenagers could possibly be bored with their world. The culture in which they live is far more exciting and stimulating than that experienced by previous generations. Whereas we grew up with little streets containing small toyshops, they have grown up with shopping malls containing massive Toys R Us superstores. Whereas we had a couple of swings and a roundabout in the corner of a muddy field, they have huge theme parks such as Alton Towers and Disney World. Whereas the extent of our sporting opportunities was usually a short swim up and down the municipal baths, they can go to fully equipped sports centres offering everything from archery to tai kwon do. Whereas TV offered us few programmes relevant to our age, on small black and white televisions, they can watch non-stop, 24-hour, high-colour, youth television on MTV and other cable channels – not to mention video and satellite.

And yet they are bored! Parents of teenagers know that one of the phrases they often hear from their children is 'I'm bored.' And if parents venture to suggest any activity to their teenager this may be dismissed with the response, 'Nah, that's boring.' Such boredom can lead teenagers into terribly damaging and self-destructive behaviour.

In 1994 the *Daily Mail* ran a news story about an 18-year-old boy. On the surface he seemed to have everything going for him. He was successful in his studies. He had obtained excellent GCSE grades. He was doing well on a new computer course at college. He also had some good friends and a loving girlfriend. But he often moaned, 'I'm bored.' One night, after drinking four pints of lager, and complaining that he could 'still taste life', he walked to a nearby railway track and laid his head on the line. When they found his body, just inches away from it was his last word, chalked on a stone. It said, 'BORED'.

Paula was 15 years old when she was interviewed by *New Internationalist* magazine.[25] She talked freely about her heroin addiction, and how she now works as a prostitute to fund her habit. When asked why so many young people take drugs, she replied, '. . . because there's nowt to do . . . give us more to occupy us kids so we don't get so bored.' We might, quite justifiably, reply, 'How much more do you want? How on earth can you be bored when today's world offers you so much that you can do?'

Isn't this the most exciting world that any generation has grown up in? Through the development of computers, for the price of a local phone call we can immediately share images and information with someone in another country. Our stereos can play any music we want to hear, at any time, at any volume. Our TVs can show us events as they happen, anywhere in the world.

Meanwhile scientists are making new discoveries and creating new inventions with dazzling speed. This is the era of nanotechnology and virtual reality. Everything seems to be moving at a breathless pace. And today's teenagers are the very first generation to grow up within it. Yet they are bored. Why is this? It is because this fast-paced, non-stop, multimedia world has brought with it a problem – in fact two problems which compound one another.

First, when someone grows up in the middle of this exciting world, they tend to develop an expectation that they must always be excited. They don't expect to be bored. They don't view boredom simply as an inevitable fact of life, something that we can't avoid, and must learn to cope with. Rather, they develop the idea that boredom means that something has gone wrong. If they are bored, this is a problem and it must be dealt with. Something must be done to make life exciting again – because life must never be boring.

Second, when people experience a new level of excitement, their excitement threshold tends to increase. However exciting something may be when they first experience it, once they have been there, and done that, it tends to lose its excitement value – it may even become boring. So they need something else which is higher, or faster, or brighter, or louder to excite them – so that they are not bored.

We can see an example of this in the continual development of rollercoaster rides. One is high, so the next one has to be higher. Then one is steep, so the next one has to be even steeper. As the Roller-Coaster Club of Great Britain says in its publicity, 'The more terrifying, the more daring, the more death-defying the rollercoaster is, the more popular it becomes.' There was a time when the rollercoasters at Thorpe Park or Alton Towers produced the pinnacle of excitement, but these soon began to feel tame. So people headed for the Pepsi Max Big One at Blackpool, which ran at 76 miles per hour down its 205-foot drop, angled at sixty-five degrees. In time, that too lost its edge, so people longed for Fujiyama in Japan, with its 239-foot drop, running at 86 miles per hour, or for the Ultra Twister in Texas, with its eighty-five degree angles. And so today the story continues in a never ending quest to go faster, higher and steeper.

Today's TV producers and advertisers have clearly identified this problem. How can they interest people in their programme or their product? It has to grip people. It cannot be boring. So it must be more exciting than the last programme, or the last product. Thus, to beat it, MTV becomes faster and brighter; soaps become more traumatic; films become more violent; and the adverts tell us that drinking a can of cola is far more exciting than free-fall parachuting or snowboarding or shark wrestling. This strategy works, in the short term. But it also continues to push up the excitement threshold. Millions of pounds are spent on programmes and adverts which are ultimately self-defeating. The TV producers and advertising agencies simply keep moving their own goal posts.

Understood in this way we can see why drugs are so appealing to the generation that has grown up in this fast-paced, multi-media, exciting world. If a teenager has an expectation that she should not be bored, and yet she keeps getting bored, she will find a drug-induced buzz very attractive. If external activities cannot give the rush, why not get it internally? If one cannot feel a buzz indirectly through the things one does or watches or hears, why not get that feeling directly through chemicals? Thus drugs provide the experience of excitement and fulfilment that many teenagers have grown up to expect and yet never seem to find. They will give the rush, the pleasure, the thrill. They will banish the boredom.

I have never taken any illicit drugs in my life, and I don't want to. But I have talked to enough drug users to understand how powerfully attractive they are. Some anti-drug campaigners try to tell us that whereas medicine is taken by people who are ill and it makes them feel better, a drug is taken by people who are well and it makes them feel ill. When people say such things, they do not seem to understand what drugs do for the user. Drugs do not make them feel ill. They make them feel good. In fact they make them feel great – for a while. Those of us who have never used drugs look from the outside and see only the shaking, the sweating, the delirium, the risk, the mess, the death. But things look and feel very different for the user.

If you find this difficult to understand, I recommend that you read the novel *Trainspotting*.[26] This best selling book by Irvine Welsh tells the story of a group of young heroin addicts who will do anything to get their fix.

The squalor and degradation is graphically described right from the start. Within the first few pages we find the main character, Mark Renton, in a toilet at the back of a crowded betting shop. The bowl is blocked and the mess has overflowed onto the floor, where others have added to it by standing at the door and simply urinating into the room. Mark is kneeling in the deep pool of urine, which is soaking up into his clothes. He has his hand down the blocked toilet bowl and he is hunting through other people's half dissolved faeces in order to rescue his opium suppositories which have just come out with his diarrhoea. Eventually he finds them. He wipes them off as best he can. Then, because he is worried about losing them out of his bottom again, he considers eating them instead.

Reading this, and looking from the outside as we do, we may wonder how anyone could ever possibly live like that. An experience such as this seems so repulsive and revolting that we think it must surely put anyone off using drugs for ever. But that is to misunderstand what goes on in the mind of the drug user. For them it is not repulsive or revolting. They feel detached from the stench, the mess, the degradation. They feel great.

Trainspotting illustrates this by telling us the story through the eyes of the drug user himself. Renton describes the effects of heroin by saying, 'Take yir best orgasm, multiply the feeling by twenty, and you're still f***ing miles off the pace.' Things may look repulsive to us on the outside, but to them on the inside it's a very different story.

So it is for teenagers who take drugs to overcome their boredom. They certainly work. If the teenagers of the future continue to believe that they must never be bored, and if their excitement threshold continues to be raised, then we should not be surprised if they continue to take drugs.

If we are to deal with the powerful attraction of drugs, we must tackle this problem of boredom. We will consider how we might do that in Chapter 7. But, before that, we must consider the other major underlying reasons why teenagers take drugs – to join in with friends and to deal with the pain in their lives.

Joining in With Their Friends

As we have already discovered, and will continue to see throughout this book, whatever aspect of teenage behaviour we seek to understand, it is so important that we look beyond the simple, superficial answers that have often been given, and accepted, in the past. In considering what it means for teenage drug users to 'join in with their friends', we will find that this is no exception.

There is a traditional, simple and superficial explanation for drug abuse in terms of 'peer pressure'. According to this view, teenagers take drugs because they want to fit in with others around them. Their friends are taking drugs, so they follow. There is no doubt that peer pressure is a motivating factor in some teenage behaviour. However, if we think that 'joining in with their friends' is all about peer pressure and peer pressure alone, we will miss a much deeper and much more important underlying factor.

When teenagers talk about taking drugs in order to join in with their friends, most of them do not mean that they are blindly following the lead of other people. Rather they are referring to the fact that they are seeking to be part of a community which, together, experiences something beyond the limitations of the normal physical world.

Of course most teenagers will not express it in that way. As with many aspects of teenage behaviour the young people themselves may not have thought through their motives consciously, nor be able to articulate them clearly. However, some have, particularly those who use ecstasy, and it is well worth listening to them.

A teenage girl who is heavily into ecstasy and the dance scene was interviewed on TV. She explained why she used drugs and, in particular, described the experience of joining with a group of people who all take ecstasy and then dance together. 'The only thing that matters is what's going on at the moment,' she said, 'and the thing that's going on at the moment is just intense happiness and having a good time. Everybody around you is sharing the same experience – it's very much a collective social thing. You're aware that there are other people across the country doing exactly the same as you, having the same experience. It's good to be part of something that feels that good.'

On the same TV programme a boy said, 'Taking an E makes everyone seem so close, happy and peaceful. It's like finding a part of yourself you'd forgotten you had. A rave is a spiritual experience, our hearts beat as one.' Ecstasy was once called the 'love drug' because of the way in which it removes emotional barriers and inhibitions. It increases the user's awareness, sensitivity and confidence. This is particularly heightened when it is used in a dance club, where hundreds, perhaps thousands, of young people join together in a collective experience of music, lights and dance through the night. In this setting, ecstasy produces a feeling of togetherness, a sense of community. It induces a collective experience that transcends the normal bounds of this world.

That is why some people describe it as a spiritual community experience. As one put it, 'Going to a rave is like going to church. Someone stands out the front and everyone listens to him. We all need someone to follow. We're just like a congregation – we dance and shout and then afterwards we get together in groups and talk about the experience. We open up our hearts and souls to each other.'

Such a spiritual community experience is very attractive to a generation that is looking for a community to which they can belong.

Searching for Community

Today's teenagers have grown up through the greatest sociological upheaval of all time. In the last few decades the most fundamental fixed points of our society have disintegrated. Whether we look at marriage, the nuclear family, the extended family, schools and universities, or the wider community in general, we find that previously stable structures in the lives of young people have fragmented. Many of today's teenagers, who have lived their formative years during this time of upheaval, are in consequence desperately looking for some kind of community to which they can belong.

Just thirty years ago, when I was a teenager, it was considered a terrible scandal if a couple decided that they would live together without getting married. It was called 'living in sin' and very few people did it. However, since then, things have changed markedly. Increasing numbers of couples decide that they will not marry. Between 1983 and 1993 the number of marriages in the UK fell by 25 per cent.[27] Since then the trend seems to have accelerated. Marriage figures from the UK Office for National Statistics show a drop from 182,000 in 1993 to 174,000 in 1994. Over the subsequent decade marriage rates have decreased further, with the lowest number since 1987 observed in 2001. The UK Office for National Statistics identified the most pronounced decline during the period 1992 to 2002 in marriages that were the first for both parties and for those aged under 30 years.[28] This is not a peculiarly British phenomenon. In the United States, the Census Bureau survey of 1990 found that there were 4.2 million unmarried couples living together.

Many of those who do get married are pessimistic about the length of time that they will remain together. A 1990 survey[29] revealed that 40 per cent of engaged couples do not expect their marriage to last – indeed, 5 per cent of brides and 4 per cent of grooms are unfaithful to their fiancé in the time before their wedding. Then, tragically, the divorce statistics show that many of their expectations are fulfilled. And this is a growing trend. National divorce statistics in 2004 show an increase of 3.7 per cent from the previous year. This is the highest number since 1996,[30] when at least four out of every ten new marriages ended in divorce.[31]

As marriage has disintegrated over recent years, so has the nuclear family. According to figures from the UK Office for National Statistics, in 1985 just over 19 per cent of babies were born to parents who were not married. By 1995 that figure had risen to almost 34 per cent. By 2000 that figure had risen further to nearly 47 per cent. For 15–19-year-olds the proportion of first births outside marriage had increased from under 50 per cent in 1980 to over 90 per cent in 2000.[32] Some of these babies are born to cohabiting parents who intend to stay together permanently, but many are not. Furthermore, of those who are born in wedlock, many find that their parents subsequently divorce. It has been estimated that, every day, approximately 400 children in the UK watch their family split up.

When I was at primary school everyone in my class had a mummy and a daddy with whom they lived. I had never heard of the word 'divorce', let alone understood what it meant. When I moved up to secondary school, one boy in my class told us that his parents had separated. To the rest of us this seemed really strange. We couldn't comprehend it. Twenty years later, when my son went to primary school, he found that many of his classmates lived only with their mummy (and a few lived only with their daddy), while others were trying to live through their parents' divorce. If present trends continue children who still live with both parents may become a minority group.

There are those who seem to think that we are better off without the nuclear family. They argue that the idea of a mum and dad living together with their children is just a social convention which is now out-dated. But that isn't what the teenagers I work with tell me. For them their parents' divorce is devastating. They want to live with both their mum and their dad. This isn't just socially conditioned – it is biologically conditioned. Each one of them was conceived by a mum and a dad together. They couldn't be conceived by a single mum or a single dad on their own, nor by a cohabiting homosexual couple. It took their mum and their dad together to bring them into existence. So they naturally want the two people who conceived them to care for them throughout their growing years. They want to know that their mum and dad will be together bringing them up as they were together conceiving them. If this doesn't happen they often feel rejected and unwanted.

And yet over the last few decades the nuclear family has disintegrated at an alarming rate. This, in turn, has had a corresponding effect upon the wider, extended family. When parents divorce and one moves out to live in another house this not only disrupts the relationship that children have with that parent, but also the relationships with their grandparents, aunts, uncles and cousins. Increasingly, grandparents of children from broken families are reporting that they find it very hard to maintain their contact with those grandchildren that now live with their ex-daughter-in-law or ex-son-in-law. And the same applies to aunts, uncles, nephews and nieces.

This break-up of the extended family due to divorce adds to the break-up which is due to the changes in education and employment opportunities in recent years.

In past generations, the members of an extended family usually all lived in the same town. They would spend much of their lives together. As each child grew up they would go to a local school and then move on to a local job, typically joining their relations to work in the same factory, dockyard or steelworks.

In recent decades, however, education has increasingly extended beyond the school years to college and university. For many students, this has meant travelling away from home to live in another city. At the same time the demands of the job market have meant that many, of all ages, have found themselves being required to move in order to secure employment.

Consequently, the members of extended families have been spread all over the country. They may get together again for a short time at special events but these once tightly knit communities have, over the decades, become increasingly fragmented.

In more recent years another form of fragmentation has taken place in many teenagers' experience of community. This is due to the changes taking place in schools and colleges.

In the middle of the 1980s I began working in the colleges of Hampshire, as a sort of roving chaplain. At that time these colleges were vibrant communities in which teenagers would spend their whole day, not just studying but also taking part in a wide range of extra-curricular activities, or simply sitting in the common room discussing the big questions of life. In recent years, however, the colleges have been restructured. Now many students attend the college only for their lessons and there may not even be a common room any more. In the space of a few years many colleges have turned from educational communities, where students felt that they belonged, into educational supermarkets where students go for a few hours each day to purchase their educational goods. As they do so they may talk to the teacher on the counter and a few of the other students in the checkout queue but generally they have very little contact with the other shoppers. Here again their community has become fragmented.

If we then look beyond families and schools to the wider aspects of society, we find that these are also increasingly geared to the individual rather than the community.

The growth of technology fuels this, as we can now shop by computer, and bank by computer, and be entertained by a computer. Internet chat lines enable computer users to develop 'friendships' with people they never meet, and whose real names they never know. It seems as if there is a drive to replace the flesh and blood reality of other people with a computer-based virtual reality. As an advert for a certain hand-held computer game put it, 'Not got any friends? Don't worry, with this game you don't need friends.'

But we do need friends. Whatever technology can do for us, something in us cries out for community. We need somewhere stable where we can belong. This is particularly the case for young people.

Is this not partly the reason for the success of the TV soaps? Every day teenagers will stare into their television sets to watch the communities that seem to exist in Ramsay Street, or Emmerdale, or Brookside, or Albert Square. These appeal to young people who want to be a part of a community, to a generation who are desperate for somewhere to belong. And yet they are not real. They cannot be truly satisfying. So teenagers continue to look elsewhere for their experience of community.

The French scholar Michel Maffesoli has written[33] about the growth of what he calls 'neo-tribalism'. He says that this occurs where individuals are desperately searching for community and so they group together and sport the symbolic tags of tribal allegiance. For today's teenagers this may be a particular TV soap, or a special trainer, or a designer label. But, as Maffesoli points out, these neo-tribes are not the stable communities that the ancient tribes were. Membership is easily revocable. Thus the neo-tribes are transient and always in flux.

Consequently such attempts to create a community always fail to be satisfying. The British sociologist Zygmunt Bauman writes[34] of 'imagined communities' which exist only through occasional outbursts of togetherness. Thus one might think of football matches, demonstrations and festivals as imagined communities, where attempts are made to replace the permanent experience of community with temporary community events.

Once again these imagined communities cannot meet our deepest need for a real community to which we belong. Therefore, just as we saw that some teenagers take drugs in order to deal chemically with their boredom, so some teenagers take drugs in order to deal chemically with their search for community.

For them, ecstasy promises to deliver the experience of community that they long for. They may not feel that there is anywhere for them to belong in their family, their school or even elsewhere in society. But, when they take ecstasy and join hundreds of others to dance through the night, at last they can feel that they have found a true community of which they can be a member. They have found somewhere to belong.

However, this ecstasy-induced experience is itself only another one of Maffesoli's neo-tribes, another one of Bauman's imagined communities. These young people haven't really found a true experience of community – just a drug-induced illusion, a chemical con. And when the drug wears off, they are, once more, on their own – looking for somewhere to belong, feeling the pain of their loneliness.

The desperation of such isolation adds to the other sources of pain that teenagers experience in their lives. They want something to deal with the pain. So they turn again to drugs to try to anaesthetise themselves. And they look for other ways in which they might block out the pain rather more permanently – as we will consider in the next chapter.

Notes

[1] 'Drug Use, Smoking and Drinking Among People in England in 2003'. National Statistics. A survey on behalf of the Department of Health by the National Centre for Social Research and the National Foundation for Educational Research.

[2] *British Medical Journal*, Vol. 315, No. 7103, August 1997.

[3] 'Drug Use, Smoking and Drinking Among Young Teenagers'. National Statistics. Department of Health, 2003.

[4] 'Monitoring the Future: National Institutes of Health', US Department of Health and Human Services, University of Michigan, 2004.

[5] 'Children and Young People: Substance Misuse Services', HMSO, 1996.

[6] 'Young People in 2004', Schools Health Education Unit.

[7] *The Times*: 5 June 2005.

[8] 'Cannabis Use in Adolescence and Risk for Adult Psychosis: longitudinal prospective study'. L. Arseneault et al. *British Medical Journal*, November 2002.

[9] 'Knowledge and Experience of Drug Use Among Church-Affiliated Young People', *Evangelical Alliance*, 1996.

[10] 'National Study of Youth and Religion', University of North Carolina, 2002.

[11] 'Drug Use, Smoking and Drinking Among Young Teenagers'. National Statistics. Department of Health, 2003.

[12] Survey by the National Center on Addiction and Substance Abuse at Columbia University, 1996.

[13] Survey by The National Center on Addiction and Drug Abuse at Columbia University, 2003.

[14] *The Sunday Times*, 2 February, 1997.

[15] N. McKegancy et al. 'Preteen Children and Illegal Drugs'. In *Drugs: Education, Prevention and Policy*, 2004.

[16] *Daily Mail*, 23 September 2004.

[17] See Plato's *Republic*.

[18] Survey by The National Center on Addiction and Substance Abuse, Columbia University, 2003.

[19] 'Young People in 2004'. Schools Health Education Unit.

[20] Survey by The National Center on Addiction and Substance Abuse at Columbia University, 1996.

[21] Reported in *The Times*, 23 October 1996.

[22] Survey by The National Center on Addiction and Substance Abuse, Columbia University, 1996.

[23] To be more precise they cited boredom and stress. Clearly teenagers face stress about many issues: exams, employment prospects, their image, their relationships, their developing sexuality. We will look at some of these stress factors in other chapters, but here I want to concentrate on the boredom aspect.

[24] Survey by The National Center on Addiction and Substance Abuse, Columbia University, 2003.

[25] *New Internationalist*, July 1997.

[26] I. Welsh, *Trainspotting*, Mandarin, 1994.

[27] 'Marriage and Divorce Statistics', 1993, Office of Population, Censuses and Surveys, HMSO, 1995.

[28] 'Annual Update 2005: Population Trends 119', Office for National Statistics.

[29] *Wedding and Home*, 1990.

[30] Divorces: National Statistics 2004.

[31] 'Population Trends 83', Office of Population Census and Surveys, HMSO, 1996.

[32] 'Annual Update 2005: Population Trends 119', Office for National Statistics.

[33] M. Maffesoli, 'Jeux de Masques', in *Design Issues IV*, 1988.

[34] Z. Bauman, *Intimations of Post-modernity*, Routledge, 1992.

Chapter 3

I Feel Like Giving Up

*I feel permanently low, I'm not sleeping well and
I'm having problems at school. I can't cope any
more . . .*

FROM A LETTER TO *MIZZ*, A TEENAGE MAGAZINE

*One morning you wake up – afraid that you are
going to live.*

ELIZABETH WURTZEL[1]

Kurt Cobain was a very happy young child. His mother
says that 'he got up every morning with such joy that
another day was to be had'. He was well known in the
town where he grew up, particularly for his habit of
marching down the street, banging his toy drum and
singing 'Hey Jude' at the top of his voice.

Everything changed, however, when Kurt was eight
years old. His Mum and Dad separated. 'It just completely destroyed his life,' said his Mum later. He
plunged into a depression from which he never seemed
able to escape. Even when his band, Nirvana, became
hugely successful he could not be happy. Some days he

would lock himself in the recording studio and just let out loud screams into the microphone. He developed stomach pains that the doctors were unable to diagnose or resolve. He took illicit drugs in an attempt to dull the physical ache in his body and the emotional pain in his soul. But the pain in his life was so powerful that in the end he bought a gun and killed himself. This is a tragically familiar pattern with too many teenagers.

I had spent a hard day in a college, where I was speaking at a series of events, and had just popped into my office to pick up the post when the phone rang. 'It's Mrs Cole here,' said a trembling voice. 'I'm sorry to bother you, but it's Lucy, there's something wrong with her and she won't tell me what it is. She is asking for you. Can you come over? She says you'll need to come straight away. Nick, I'm really worried about her.'

So was I. I had got to know Lucy quite well over recent months. I was aware of some of the problems with which she was struggling. I knew that her mum and dad had just separated. I knew that she was falling behind with her college work. I knew that she was madly in love with a boy who was now not at all interested in her. I knew something of the turmoil that she was experiencing. Most of all I knew that she didn't want to live through the pain that she felt right now.

'I'm coming straight away,' I told Mrs Cole, and put the phone down. I ran to my car and drove as fast as I could across the town. My mind was racing and my stomach was churning. What had Lucy done? Why wouldn't she tell her mum? Should I have told Mrs Cole to call an ambulance? Or was I just overreacting?

I pulled up my car in front of their house, jumped out and ran up the drive. I tried to appear calm as Mrs Cole met me at the door and took me in to Lucy – who was clearly very distressed.

'I just don't want to go on any more,' she sobbed. 'I've had enough.'

I sat down next to her and asked her what she had done.

She took a deep breath and continued, 'I've taken a load of tablets.'

It was just as I had feared.

That was some years ago. Lucy is now happily married, with her own young family. But she could so easily have been yet another statistic on the mounting list of teenage suicides.

According to the Samaritans[2] the number of attempted suicides by young people doubled over a 10-year period. There are now around 24,000 cases of attempted suicides by adolescents (10–19 years) each year in England and Wales, which is a horrifying one attempt every 20 minutes.[3] Not all who attempt suicide are effective (nor do they all mean to be), but many are. In the USA, 12 per cent of all deaths among 10–24-year-olds result from suicide, following behind only road traffic accidents (32 per cent), homicide (15 per cent) and other intentional injuries (12 per cent).[4] Suicide by young males is in particular, an increasingly serious public health issue. In the UK, the suicide rate for older male teenagers almost doubled between 1970 and 1988, remaining high through the 1990s.[5]

The fact that any teenager should take his own life is a great tragedy. The fact that the number of teenagers doing so has risen over the last few decades should make us very concerned. The statistics must surely motivate us to find all the reasons for this, and to deal with them.

The figures for teenage suicide have not only been climbing but also widening. Suicides amongst younger teenagers used to be quite rare, but now they are increasing. A study by the John Hopkins School of Public

Health[6] revealed that the suicide rate for 10–14-year-olds doubled in the years 1980 to1985. Data from the National Institute of Mental Health in 2001 revealed that the suicide rate for 10–14-year-olds was now 1.3/100,000 compared to 7.9/100,000 in 15–19-year-olds.[7]

And these are only the figures for effective suicides. We must also be aware that many other teenagers make serious attempts at suicide, or inflict other forms of harm on themselves.

A study from the Centre for Disease of Control and Prevention in 1999[8] revealed that 8.3 per cent of American teenagers had attempted suicide at least once during the preceding year and the figures are similar in Great Britain. The statistics for self-harm are even greater. One cannot obtain comprehensive figures for the number of teenagers that deliberately hurt themselves, since many of them do it in such a way that they don't require hospital treatment. However, it is estimated[9] that, for every teenager who commits suicide, about thirty harm themselves in some other way.

As these statistics for suicides, suicide attempts and other forms of self-harm increase we must also take account of the number of potential suicides that may be waiting in the wings. A recent survey of 13,000 school pupils[10] aged between 13 and 15 found that 27 per cent of them had considered taking their own life. An American study of high-school children reported that one in five teenagers had seriously contemplated suicide, more than 1 in 6 had made plans to end their life and more than 1 in 12 had actually made a suicide attempt.[11]

These are not just statistics in a research report. They are real people. They may be your child, your niece, your nephew, or a pupil in your class. I meet them regularly in my work with teenagers.

Judy came from a really good home. Her parents

clearly loved one another and their children. In fact, they seemed to love all people, even those who were quite unlovely. Uncle Bill was one of those. He wasn't actually Judy's uncle, he was just a neighbour, but Judy's mum and dad had given him that title to make him feel accepted in the family. They also gave him their daughter, Judy, to visit him and take him cakes. They didn't understand why she never seemed keen to go to Bill's house. And she couldn't tell them. She didn't really understand what happened when she was there but she knew it was something wrong and she thought it must be her fault.

It was many years before Judy told anyone that Uncle Bill had been sexually abusing her. Judy felt spoilt, unclean and messed up. 'It hurt,' she said. 'It still hurts.'

As she grew into her teenage years, Judy started using cannabis in an attempt to deal with the pain. In the years that followed she progressed through a range of drugs, eventually starting on heroin. But these only numbed the pain for a little while. She began to think about stopping the pain altogether. Over the next few years she made several suicide attempts. 'I just don't feel like living any more,' she said. 'Nothing could make me feel right again. I just want to get rid of the pain for ever.'

I have tried to help many teenagers like Judy. We don't have to look very far to see why they want to take drugs or even to take their own life. They want to deal with the pain in their lives, and the source of that pain is very clear. A survey[12] of people who had deliberately taken an overdose found that 67 per cent gave the reason that 'the situation was so unbearable that I had to do something and didn't know what else to do'.

However, there are other teenagers who resort to drugs or suicide, without there appearing to be such an obvious reason. Claire was one of these. She spent many of her teenage years stealing valium from her mother and contemplating her own suicide. In fact she made several suicide attempts – not really meaning to kill herself at that point but just proving to herself that she could if she wanted to.

Claire knew that there was no one incident that had caused her distress. She hadn't been abused like Judy. Her family had not broken up like Kurt Cobain's. She just felt that she couldn't cope. She didn't feel like going on. The doctors told her that she was suffering from clinical depression.

One might be tempted to think that what we have seen so far in this chapter provides all the explanation we need for one of the reasons behind teenage drug abuse and teenage suicide. Clearly it does provide a good explanation. Some teenagers, like Judy, take drugs or attempt suicide as a way of dealing with the pain in their life which comes from specific bad experiences. Others, like Claire, take drugs or attempt suicide as a way of dealing with the feeling of pain in their life which comes from medical problems such as depression. If this explains it all, then the solutions may seem to be equally apparent. Thus people like Judy are usually offered counselling and people like Claire are usually offered medication.

However, as true as these specific explanations may be, they don't seem to be the whole story. For one thing they don't account for the rise in drug abuse and teenage suicide. Why is it that the figures should be rising as they are? Is there another factor that has been overlooked? I believe that there is. We must look more deeply and consider the possibility that there may be a more fundamental reason for these particular responses to pain.

I would propose that recent medical developments have brought about a new attitude to pain and sickness among many of today's young generation, which means that, instead of enduring pain and sickness and learning to cope with it, they tend to seek a quick solution to it – even if this means resorting to drugs or suicide.

To explore this we must begin by looking back at some events in history. Once again you may initially wonder what on earth some of this has to do with the problems of teenage drug abuse and suicide. But stick with me.

An Anaesthetic Age

A small group of people had some very strange parties back in the 1840s. For a short time it became fashionable to pass round a pig's bladder containing a special gas for the partygoers to inhale. The chemical name for the gas was nitrous oxide, but it was better known at parties as 'laughing gas'. It was given that name because of the effect it had upon the person who inhaled it. Once they had breathed it in they became light-headed and giggly, as if they were drunk. Then they became very sleepy, and if they inhaled enough they would pass out.

Gradually doctors and dentists began to develop an interest in the effects that this gas could produce. For many centuries they had tried to use drugs of various kinds in an attempt to reduce the pain and distress of surgery, but none had ever been very successful.

The Greek poet Homer wrote about nepenthe which was used in his time. We don't know exactly what this was, but it was possibly a form of cannabis. The Arabian doctors tried using *Hyoscyamus*. This biennial plant which grows wild on waste ground contains the crystalline substance known as atropine – which is still used in modern medicine to dilate the pupils for retinal examinations. For many years the surgeons on British ships usually gave a big slug of rum to any unfortunate sailors who had to have their legs or arms amputated.

None of these attempts at pain relief were very good. So the patient simply had to endure the agony while the doctors worked as quickly as they could. There are records of one surgeon working so fast that, as well as amputating his patient's leg (which was his intention), he also took off one of his patient's testicles and two of his assistant's fingers. No matter how fast the surgeon worked, this was clearly a very painful process – and the patient simply had to bite the bullet and put up with it.

But in the nineteenth century, nitrous oxide, and some other substances, seemed to offer the possibility of an effective anaesthetic. In 1799, some years before laughing gas became popular at those parties, the 21-year-old chemist Humphrey Davy had inhaled it as an experiment and discovered that it had anaesthetic properties. At the time no one had been interested. Some fifty years later, however, doctors and dentists began to try using it in their operations.

In 1845 Horace Wells, an American dentist, attempted a public demonstration of the use of nitrous oxide anaesthesia for dental extractions. The demonstration was unsuccessful, but he did cause other medical practitioners to begin experimenting with this gas, and with other substances, such as ether and chloroform.

In 1846 William Morton, another American dentist, administered ether to a patient having a neck tumour removed at the Massachusetts General Hospital in Boston. The success of this anaesthetic convinced the medical world that general anaesthesia was a practical proposition. Gradually anaesthetics became more widely used. In Britain, Queen Victoria gave her official stamp of approval to the use of anaesthesia when she gave birth to her eighth child, Prince Leopold, in 1853. She allowed her physician, John Snow, to give her chloroform, and the delivery was successful.

Since those early experimental days, anaesthetics have become increasingly sophisticated and gradually more available to all of us in the West.

Today, it is true to say that we live in an anaesthetic age. If we are admitted into hospital for surgery we will find a dedicated anaesthetist who will give us trichloroethylene or halothane to ensure that we feel no pain. If we go to the dentist for even a small filling we will be given an injection of lignocaine to ensure that the nerves of the tooth are numbed. If we pull a muscle we will be given ibuprofen. If we have a headache we can take an aspirin or a paracetamol.

Whatever medical problem we face, this anaesthetic age tells us 'you should not feel pain'. It even seems to tell us 'you should not feel discomfort.' The process of fixing the tubes through which the modern surgical anaesthetics are delivered is uncomfortable. So the anaesthetic age deals with this by giving us an injection of the barbiturate sodium thiopental so that we are relaxed and asleep before the tubes are put in place. Thus, even the discomfort of having the pain taken away is itself taken away.

Now don't get me wrong. I love anaesthetics. I don't like pain. If I need surgery I will be so thankful that anaesthesia has been invented. I am not, for one minute, suggesting that we should get rid of anaesthetics, nor make them less universally available.

What I am saying is that we need to be aware of the underlying effect that this anaesthetic age seems to have upon those who are growing up in it. Particularly on many of today's teenagers. If we grow up in an anaesthetic age we will tend to develop an implicit expectation that none of us should ever feel pain at all.

When I was 13 years old I had to have a lot of fillings

put in my teeth. I vividly remember those visits to the dentist. For some of my fillings I was given an injection, but for others I wasn't. I had to learn to put up with a certain amount of pain. If I had lived more than a hundred years ago I would not have had any anaesthetic for anything that was done on my teeth. I would simply have had to learn to endure the pain.

However, today's teenagers have not grown up in the world of a hundred years ago, or even the world that I knew. They have grown up in an anaesthetic age. That is all that they have known. So many of them have absorbed the idea that they should not feel pain. If they do experience any, they will tend to seek to have that pain taken away.

A Sanitised Society

Furthermore, not only is this an anaesthetic age, it is also a sanitised society. The world in which we live tends to give us the idea that we should not experience sickness or death.

In past generations, when people were sick they were treated at home. No matter how ill they became, they would be kept in the family house. Even when they died, they would die at home. Their children would watch them get weaker. They would even gather round and watch them die.

Today, however, when people are very ill they are often taken away to hospital. The children may visit them, but only for a little while. Some parents decide not even to let the child come to the hospital, in case they become distressed by the sights and smells of disease. When the sick person dies, some children may see the death, or visit the dead body, but that is increasingly rare.

I know this from some surveys I have conducted. I spend a lot of my time in schools and colleges helping teenagers to explore spiritual and moral issues. When we look at the question of suffering I sometimes ask them whether they have ever watched anyone die – in real life, I mean, not on the TV. The result is very consistent, wherever I am. Very few of today's teenagers have ever been with someone when they have died, or have even seen a dead body.

If I had asked the same question a hundred or even fifty years ago I would no doubt have found a very different answer. Indeed if I were to ask the same question in many African villages today the teenagers would look at me as if I were very strange. 'What a funny question to ask,' they would probably say. 'Of course we've seen lots of dead bodies.'

So, today's teenagers are growing up not only in an anaesthetic age, but also in a sanitised society, a world in which sickness and death are often hidden from them. Thus many of them unconsciously absorb the idea that they should not expect to feel pain or to experience sickness. If they do, then it is not a normal part of life to be put up with; it is something that has gone wrong and so must be dealt with.

In my work I meet many different people. So I am frequently saying, 'Hello, how are you?' I notice, when I do this, that there is usually a very big difference between the answers given by people of different generations. Older people invariably say, 'I'm fine, thank you.' They reply this way even if they are clearly not fine at all. I recently met the mother of a teenager whom I had been helping. When I asked her how she was she replied in the usual way, saying, 'I'm fine'. This was despite the fact that she was in a wheelchair at the time, clearly in considerable pain from a back injury she had just sustained. However, when I asked her daughter the same question I was given a very different answer. She replied, 'I feel really rough, I think I've got flu.' She clearly hadn't got flu. She just had a slight sniffle. But to her it seemed a big illness.

I have lost count of how many students tell me that they think they have caught glandular fever, when really they have just experienced some of the normal aches and pains of life. A survey by the Schools Health Education Unit revealed that 52 per cent of 14–15-year-old females and 29 per cent of males reported taking a painkiller on at least one day in the previous week.[13] Many teenagers seem to be very alert to the slightest pain. They do seem to expect that they should never feel pain or experience sickness. Isn't this the result of growing up in an anaesthetic age and a sanitised society?

Physical and Emotional Pain

But all teenagers do feel pain. Many of them feel lots of it. Because there is more than one type of pain. Physical pain is bad enough, but emotional pain is perhaps even worse. The pain of seeing your parents divorce and your family fall apart is just as great, if not greater, than the pain of surgery or dentistry.

Similarly they do get sick and die. Sometimes not physically, but emotionally. The heartbreak of being rejected feels like a sickness. The experience of abuse makes the victim feel as if some part of them has died.

Paradoxically, in modern society, as physical pain has been taken away, so the sources of emotional pain seem to have increased. As we noted in the last chapter, Western society has become increasingly fragmented. Consequently, greater numbers of teenagers are experi-

enci   ain of family break-up. As we will see in the
next   , society has put people under an increasing
pressure to fit a particular image. So greater numbers of
teenagers are experiencing that sickening feeling of
inadequacy and rejection. As we will see in Chapter 5,
modern society's attitude to sex has increasingly led
many into behaviour that they later regret and which
takes a terrible toll on their lives. So greater numbers of
teenagers are experiencing the death of their self-respect.

There is no doubt that teenagers experience a lot of
pain today. And it does seem to be pain that is mainly
emotional rather than physical. But, to the person who is
experiencing it, pain is pain. We don't necessarily draw
the distinction between physical and emotional pain. So,
if we have an implicit belief that we should not feel pain and
that any experience of pain must be removed rather than
endured, then we will tend to apply that belief to emotional
pain in the same way that we do to physical pain.

This seems to be the case with many of today's
teenagers. They have grown up through an anaesthetic
age, in a sanitised society. And so they tend to have a
general expectation that they should not feel pain, whether
physical or emotional. So their experience of emotional
pain and sickness can put them in a turmoil. Many of them
don't know how to handle it. They just want to get rid of it.
Rather than enduring the pain or coping with the sickness,
they tend to look for immediate solutions. If they have a
headache they reach for the paracetamol; are we to be
surprised, then, that when they have a heartache they
reach for the cannabis or the heroin?

But the source of emotional pain cannot be dealt with
so easily. The headache may have gone when the paracetamol wears off, but the pain of a heartache will still be
there when the cannabis or heroin has finished. In fact,
when this particular anaesthetic wears off, the emotional

pain is likely to be even greater. So teenagers may try other ways to deal with their pain. But they find that none of them work. Their pain remains. It even grows. The fact that the emotional pain cannot be taken away itself becomes the source of yet more emotional pain; this can lead to an emotional spiral taking the teenager lower and lower. Nothing seems to get rid of their pain. And nothing will, except death. So suicide begins to look like a good solution. It appears to be the only remedy that will work. It offers the most effective anaesthetic. It will deal with the emotional pain for ever.

In Chapter 7 we will consider how this spiral may be broken. But next let us look at one of these sources of emotional pain – the pressure to fit a particular image.

Notes

[1] E. Wurtzel, *Prozac Nation – Young and Depressed in America: A Memoir*, Quartet Books, 1995.

[2] Reported in *The Times*, 17 May 1997.

[3] Samaritan Information Sheet 'Young People and Suicide', 2004.

[4] Grunbaum et al 2004 – Youth Risk Behaviour Surveillance – US 2003, Centres for Disease Control and Prevention.

[5] *BMJ* 2005; 330; 411–414. R. Viner and R. Booy. 'Epidemiology of health and illness'.

[6] Quoted in the *Times Educational Supplement*, 24 March 1989.

[7] National Institute of Mental Health, US, 2001.

[8] 'Youth Risk Behaviour Surveillance' – US, 1999: In CDC Surveillance Summaries, June 2000.

[9] L.J. Francis and W.K. Kray, *Teenage Religion and Values*, Gracewing, 1995.

[10] L.J. Francis and W.K. Kray, *Teenage Religion and Values*, Gracewing, 1995.

[11] Center for Disease Control and Prevention 2000: Youth Risk Behaviour Surveillance – US 1999.

[12] Quoted in M. Williams, *Cry of Pain*, Penguin, 1997.

[13] 'Young People in 2004', Schools Health Education Unit.

Chapter 4

Fitting the Image

60 per cent of 15-year-old girls want to lose weight.

JOHN BALDING[1]

80 per cent of teenage boys are unhappy with their appearance; one in four teenage boys thinks they may need cosmetic surgery.

DAILY TELEGRAPH[2]

It was just after nine o'clock when a hundred students ambled into their common room. They were going to spend the whole morning with me in one of the conferences that I run in schools and colleges across the country.

As they came in, many of them were obviously very conscious of one another. Finding the right place to sit was not just a necessity, it was also a fashion statement. They were concerned not so much with how comfortable they would be over the next three hours, but with how cool they would look. Some had to sit on the chairs provided, but most would much rather squat on a table, perch on a bench or recline on the floor – so that they

51

could pose, and strike just the right image.

Once I had been introduced I explained ..... I ...ould like them, that morning, to join with me in exploring the question of our identity and value. Who are we? What would we like to be? What do we think about our value as individual human beings? And what about the value of others?

I invited them to begin this with a guided reflection. They closed their eyes and I asked them to think about themselves – who they are and what they are like. In particular I asked them to make a mental list of the words that they would use to describe themselves. After a few moments I then asked them to imagine that I had a magic wand with which I could change people: if there was anything about themselves that they wanted altered, my magic wand could do it for them. I invited them to make a mental list of the things they would like changed.

I have carried out this exercise with many teenagers, and I find it to be a very useful one which helps them begin to gain an insight into the way in which they think about themselves. There will always be a wide range of items on their individual mental lists; and I never ask them to share their own thoughts with the group because this is a very personal and private exercise. But, through general discussion afterwards, it usually becomes clear that very many of them have used 'outside' rather than 'inside' words. When they think about themselves many of them think primarily of their external rather than their internal characteristics.

Many teenagers seem to think of themselves as big or small, fat or thin, pretty or ugly; rather than sensitive, or kind, or hurt, or stable. When they make a list of items they would like to be changed, many of them want to lose weight or have bigger muscles, less spots or a smaller nose; rather than being more peaceful, more happy, more reliable or more loving.

This is consistent with the results of other, more structured research with teenagers.

Joan Jacobs Brumberg, a professor of history at Cornell University, has reported a marked change in young girls' diaries over the past 100 years.[3] A typical entry from 1890 says, 'Resolved to work seriously, to be self-restrained in conversations and actions, not to let my thoughts wander, to be dignified, to interest myself more in others.' However a typical entry in 1990 says, 'I will try to make myself better in any way I can. I will lose weight, get new lenses, good make-up, new clothes and accessories.' Dr Brumberg notes that, whereas in the past young girls thought of 'goodness' in terms of character, they now think of it in terms of appearance.

A recent survey of 40,439 children aged between ten and fifteen, by the Schools Health Education Unit, found that 'the way you look' is the principal concern for females aged 14–15 years. Losing weight was a desire for 59 per cent of this group, and also for 53 per cent of 12–13-year-old females.[4] Another survey commissioned by the Royal College of Nursing[5] found that, of the 4,295 children aged eleven to sixteen whom they questioned, 86 per cent fretted about the way they look. Fears about being overweight, developing spots and having ugly teeth topped their list of worries. Similarly, studies in America have revealed that by the age of thirteen more than half of all American girls are unhappy with their bodies; by the age of seventeen that figure has risen to 78 per cent.[6]

Why are so many teenagers so concerned about their external appearance? Once again it is not surprising given the world in which they live. Modern culture is very image conscious – particularly modern youth culture.

The producers of TV programmes and the editors of magazines work very hard, and spend a lot of money, to ensure that their programme, or their magazine, has just the right image. That is how they become popular and attract viewers or readers. They try to catch the mood and style of the moment. They need to ensure that their magazine or TV programme fits the contemporary image.

But this is not a one-way street. TV producers and magazine editors not only respond to the mood and style of the moment, they can also have a great influence upon it. They can be part of the process that shapes the contemporary image.

In the same way, most teenagers work very hard, and spend a lot of money, to ensure that they have just the right image. They too want to be popular, they want to attract friends.

However, for them this is a one-way street. Unlike the TV producers and magazine editors, on an individual basis they are completely unable to influence the mood and style of the moment. A very small number of teenagers may be those rare people whom market researchers call 'style leaders'. But the vast majority are left simply to fit in with whatever the contemporary image may be.

It is not only teenage girls who are presented with a powerful message about the way they should look. The development of successful boy bands, and the marketing of high-profile sportsmen provides many boys with an image which they feel they ought to match. And here they face a problem. For much of the time, and certainly at the present, the contemporary image is completely unattainable for very many of them. As it is for most people.

According to research conducted at Manchester Metropolitan University[7] most women aged between 18 and 28 have measurements of at least 35-27-37. However, the average model measures 34-24-34. Similarly, the average woman is five feet, five inches high, whereas the average model is five feet, nine inches high. Sarah Beazley, who conducted the study, remarked, 'I would say that only around 5 per cent of women aged 18–28 have statistics similar to those of models.'

And yet such models are integral to the image that is presented in Western culture – particularly in teenage culture. For instance, if you look at the front covers of magazines, especially those geared for the teenage market, what do you see? You see models who fit perfectly with the style and image that our culture likes to call 'beautiful'. When did you last see a magazine with a fat, disabled, or spotty person on the cover?

When teenagers look at these magazines, what ideas do they pick up subconsciously? They cannot fail to absorb the notion that they, too, must fit this image if they are to be popular, accepted and loved. Just as a magazine is more valuable if it fits the contemporary image, so, the unconscious logic tells them, they will be more valuable if they fit with the contemporary image.

Given this state of affairs, it is not surprising that cosmetic surgery is now such a booming business. Increasing numbers of people are paying large sums to have their bodies and faces re-shaped by the scalpel or liposuction tube. Such surgery is not generally available to the average teenager. But there are other ways in which they can attempt to change their shape. Is it any wonder that so many of them develop eating disorders, such as anorexia nervosa?

This disorder typically stems from an intense fear of gaining weight, coupled with a distorted perception of one's own body image. When the anorexic youth looks in a mirror he doesn't see the reality of a painfully thin body that desperately needs more nourishment. Rather, he sees the illusion of a body that is terribly fat and desperately needs to lose more weight. The self-starvation that results can be devastating to the health of the sufferer, and some of them eventually starve themselves to death. No one knows exactly how many teenagers suffer from such eating disorders. Some research has shown that, among 15–18-year-olds, anorexia nervosa afflicts about 1 per cent of girls and 0.1 per cent of boys.[8] More recent research demonstrates that anorexia nervosa is the third most common chronic illness of adolescence.[9] However, the real number of sufferers is certain to be much greater than this since one of the major characteristics of the disorder is the desire to keep it secret – which many of them manage to do.

Jane was very thin when I met her. She had attended a summer festival where I was speaking and she seemed to attach herself to my team for the whole weekend. That enabled us to get to know one another and to talk through some quite deep issues together. I then met her several more times at various events over the next few years. On every occasion Jane looked thinner. She soon became painfully emaciated. Eventually, she confessed to me that she had effectively stopped eating. Every evening she told her parents that she had enjoyed a big meal at school and so she didn't want to eat any tea – but in reality she had not had any lunch either. In common with many who suffer from eating disorders she wanted to keep it to herself, and it was a big step forward for her to tell anyone about it. Thus began her long, slow process of recovery.

Eventually Jane began to see herself as she really was – not in comparison to some impossible image with which she tried to fit. The key for her was to begin to see herself in a new light – to look at herself differently. I helped her to recognise another image for herself, an image that was not about her external appearance but about her internal qualities.

The image that I helped Jane to consider is an image that has been largely rejected by Western culture in recent years.

Whose Image?

Psychologists tell us that there is no doubt that human beings have a powerful desire to worship someone or something outside of themselves. Whether it is the hero-worship of a 13-year-old for the 17-year-old captain of the hockey team, or the adoration of that 17-year-old for the lead singer of her favourite band, there seems to be an inherent desire within all of us to worship and adore someone or something.

This internal drive may be linked to the fact that people are instinctively religious. Wherever one travels in the world, people seem to have an inbuilt desire for God. Throughout history people have sought to find a spiritual reality beyond themselves. Looking back on his own particular spiritual search, St Augustine described it in this way: 'I carried with me only a loving memory and a desire for that of which I had the aroma but which I had not yet the capacity to eat.'[10]

If we still lived in a culture that encouraged us to seek for God we might find our spiritual fulfilment in a spiritual realm. But what happens if we grow up in a culture that has rejected God? We still want something or someone to worship. We still seek images and icons to focus upon. But where will we find them? Clearly not in heaven. So it has to be here on earth. Thus we look for people whom we can worship and adore – people whom we can strive to follow. Today's teenagers have grown up in just such a world – a world in which God has been rejected and replaced with other objects of worship.

On 31 August 1997 the world was shaken with the tragic news that Diana, Princess of Wales, had been killed in a car crash in Paris. Throughout the following week London became the focus for pilgrims travelling from all over the country to bring flowers, cards and tributes. Melvyn Bragg[11] observed that many of the inscriptions on the cards referred to Diana with 'adoration as to an idol'. Indeed, many not only echoed the statement expressed on the day of her death that 'a light had gone out in the world', but also extended it to say that 'she was the light of the world'. The messianic overtones were unmistakable. On the day after Diana's funeral, the journalist Melanie Phillips commented that the events of the week had 'shown a profound spiritual emptiness which people want to have filled'.

Indeed emptiness always will be filled, in one way or another. Thus, the reaction to Diana's tragic life and death was one example of the way in which our culture seeks and provides icons and images that we can worship and follow. Teenagers will gaze lovingly at the posters of their favourite band. Successful athletes and actors are interviewed on TV and asked for their views on moral, social or political dilemmas – not because we really think that the ability to run fast or act well qualifies them to answer these difficult questions but because somehow we have a desire to follow them and to be like them.

Thus, those we worship and follow provide for us a sense of identity, purpose and meaning. They give us an image of how we would like to be and how we think we ought to be. The images that are provided by these contemporary objects of our worship are very different from those derived from the objects of worship in past centuries.

For many years Western culture was built upon its Christian roots and the set of beliefs that stemmed from them. The Christian tradition taught us that God was our creator, it was him we should worship and it was from him that we would derive our sense of purpose, meaning and fulfilment. The explicitly clear Christian teaching about our identity told us that our image came from God, since we are all 'created in God's image'.

There was a lot of theological debate about what exactly it meant to be made in God's image. But it was always clear that this referred to our internal nature and not our external appearance. People did not believe that we look like God, but that we were created with God's nature stamped through us. That is, they believed that humans have many of God's characteristics, such as the capacity to love and be loved, to think, to feel, and to act freely. These internal characteristics were considered to be fundamental to our humanity. Thus our internal character was reckoned to be much more important than any external appearances.

However, in recent years this Christian heritage has been largely rejected. We now live in a post-Christian culture. This has had many different consequences, as we discover in later chapters of this book. But one consequence that we need to consider here concerns our belief about who we are. If the Christian belief that we are created in the image of God has been rejected, in whose image should we be? Who are we as human beings? What is our value and worth? What is our identity and meaning?

For most people the focus of our identity and meaning, our value and worth, has shifted from our internal nature to our external characteristics. As someone said recently, 'If we were created in God's image, why does everyone want to look like Halle Berry?' The fact is that our culture now does not believe that we were created in God's image, so it has replaced an internal model from God with an external model from the silver screen.

This rejection of the Christian world-view has sometimes been called 'the death of God'. The stage was set for it by the Enlightenment of the seventeenth and eighteenth centuries (see Chapter 1). Through the Enlightenment, Western culture rejected the dogma of the church. A century later Western culture rejected God himself.

The main character behind this was a German philosopher by the name of Friedrich Nietzsche. Nietzsche was born in 1844, the son of the pastor of a Lutheran church. When he was twenty he went to the University of Bonn to study theology. But Nietzsche was not to become a theologian, nor a pastor like his father. In fact, he became quite the opposite, writing books such as *The Antichrist* and *Beyond Good and Evil*. In these and his other writings, he rejected Christian belief as the product of a people who think like slaves – weak people who encourage gentleness and kindness because this serves their interests. He called people to think instead like masters who are strong and independent.

In his book *The Joyful Wisdom*, published in 1882, he expressed this belief in the phrase for which he is most well known. 'God is dead,' he wrote. 'The belief in the Christian God has become unworthy of belief.' A few years after this, Nietzsche collapsed in the streets of Turin, having lost control of his mental faculties completely. He spent the last eleven years of his life deranged, first in a Basel asylum and then in the care of his mother and sister. He died in 1900 from a paralysis probably caused by dormant tertiary syphilis.

Nietzsche ended his years as a sad, sick old man. But his ideas have lived on. They have had a profound effect upon Western culture. The *Encyclopaedia Britannica* describes him as 'certainly one of the most influential philosophers who ever lived'. His views have been a major driving force behind the march of atheism and the rejection of the foundations of Christian belief in the Western world.

A survey of 13,000 school pupils[12] aged between 13 and 15 found that only 39 per cent of them believe that God exists. And most of these do not hold to traditional Christian beliefs. This survey also showed that only 16 per cent believe that Christianity is the one true religion. The fact is that, in our post-Christian cul-ture, most people have rejected historical Christian beliefs. One of those is the belief that we are created in God's image.

It is over a hundred years since Nietzsche first wrote about the death of God. But it is only very recently that such a view has become widely accepted. Nietzsche himself recognised that this would take a long time. To him it seemed as if God was dead, but he wouldn't lie down. Nietzsche gave the name 'passive nihilism' to the fact that people did not yet realise that religious absolutes had dissolved. He said that people are bound to be reluctant to accept the death of God because to do so also means accepting that their lives are essentially purposeless and meaningless.

But here we are, some hundred years later, in a culture that does seem to have accepted Nietzsche's beliefs. Teenagers are therefore growing up in a culture through which they learn that their lives are fundamentally purposeless and meaningless – as we see when we look at the beliefs of many contemporary scientists and philosophers.

So, Who Are We?

Some try to tell us that we are simply animals. They argue that we may have evolved to a higher degree of sophistication than the other animals, but other than that there is nothing very different or special about us – we are just another form of animal. Desmond Morris, the famous zoologist, put it this way: 'There are one hundred and ninety-three living species of monkeys and apes. One hundred and ninety-two of them are covered with hair. The exception is a naked ape self-named Homo sapiens.'[13]

There are others who try to tell us that we are simply a set of chemicals and neurones. Francis Crick proposeed what he called the 'astonishing hypothesis' that 'You . . . your sense of personal identity and free-will, are in fact no more than the behaviour of a vast assembly of nerve cells and their associated molecules.'[14]

There is no doubt that our brains do contain chemicals and neurones. And these chemicals and neurones do code and carry information. Some like to use Richard Dawkins' term 'memes' for such units of information.[15] But Francis Crick and others are trying to tell us that this is all that there is. There is nothing more. There is not even a real 'me' who truly exists. Susan Blackmore, a psychologist based at the University of the West of England, has said, 'The idea that we exist is an illusion'[16] and 'The answer to the question "Who am I?" is simply "I am one of the many co-adapted meme-complexes living within this brain."'[17] Finally, others try to tell us that we are simply evolutionary by-products. Sir Fred Hoyle, the astronomer and mathematician, put it this way: '[We are] no more than ingenious machines that have evolved as strange by-products in an odd corner of the Universe.' Richard Dawkins, the evolutionist, declares that we are 'machines built by DNA whose purpose is to make more copies of the same DNA . . . [this] is every living object's sole reason for living'. According to him, the human body is created by its DNA merely so that the DNA can reproduce itself – we are a massive, but necessary digression.[18]

When launching his book *Climbing Mount Improbable*, Richard Dawkins said in a lecture,[19] 'It seems like a pointless point, and it is. . . There is no fundamental purpose in life.' At the end of his book he tells of an occasion when he was driving through the countryside with his 6-year-old daughter. They looked at the wild flowers and Dawkins asked her what she thought they were here for. She told her daddy that she thought they were here to make the world pretty and to help the bees to make honey for us. Dawkins says, 'I was touched by this and sorry that I had to tell her it wasn't true.' He thinks it isn't true because he believes that the only reason anything is here is so that it can pass on its DNA. It seems like a pointless point and it is.

He was sorry to tell her this. We can only imagine what his daughter felt to hear it. But I do know what teenagers feel when they think about such ideas, because they tell me quite frequently.

There are some who say that they wholeheartedly embrace one of these views. Such as Amanda, a very bright teenager who told me that she was a great fan of Richard Dawkins. She proudly announced her belief that we are simply biological mechanisms whose only purpose is to pass on our DNA. I tried to help her to think through what that meant for her significance and value – and the significance and value of other people in her life. In particular I asked her how she expects to react when her mother dies; will it mean nothing because her mother was only a biological mechanism that had already passed on its DNA? She said, 'I will probably cry, but that itself is only a biological reaction – it means nothing.' At least that is what Amanda said with her lips. Her eyes were telling a different story. Clearly, her heart was troubled.

So we face a crisis in our culture. Who are we? What is our value and significance? Whom should we worship and follow? We have rejected the historic Christian belief that we should worship God and try to develop God's characteristics in our lives. We have rejected the view that we are created by God in his image, with all the significance and value that this entails.

This is the world in which today's teenagers have grown up. It is the only world they have known. Those of us who are older grew up in a culture that still, broadly, held on to its Judeo-Christian heritage. We were taught about (even instructed in) Christian faith at school, and most of us went to church occasionally, if not regularly. We may have rejected Christian faith as we grew up. But the foundations were still there in our lives. Deep down we probably had, and still have, the inner sense that we are made in the image of God and that our internal character is more important than our external image.

But this is not generally so for today's teenagers. So many of them seek after and idolise other gods. They find other icons to adore. Princess Diana or Robbie Williams. And they find other images in which they wish we were made – Halle Berry, or David Beckham. It is inevitable, though, that this will lead to problems in their lives – for these gods are inadequate and unfulfilling.

The current icons of teenage culture are distant. Whereas the Christian understanding of God showed him to be available for us so that we can come to know him and experience him personally, these icons are locked away in palaces and mansions, surrounded by bodyguards who will keep the worshippers at a safe distance.

Similarly, the current images of teenage culture are unattainable. Whereas the Christian understanding that we are created in God's image brought with it the knowledge that our internal characters can become like his, the external image of the super-model will always be beyond the reach of almost all of us.

Finally, these objects of worship are so obviously faulty. Whereas the Christian understanding of God showed him to be pure and perfect, we all know of so many sports stars and pop stars who have fallen off their pedestals.

So many of today's teenagers are left with a vacuum. A vacuum filled with image rather than substance; with its focus on external appearance rather than internal character. And this inadequate filling takes its toll in their lives. It has a profound effect upon the way in which they view and treat their own bodies. As we will see in the next chapter, it also affects the way in which they view and treat the relationship between their own bodies and those of other people.

Notes

[1] J. Balding, *Young People*, University of Exeter, 1997.
[2] *Daily Telegraph*, 24 May 2005.
[3] J. Jacobs Brumberg, *The Body Project: An Intimate History of American Girls*, Random House, 1997.
[4] 'Young People in 2004', Schools Health Education Unit.
[5] Reported in *The Times*, 12 May 1997.
[6] Reported in *The Times*, 7 October 1997.
[7] Reported in *The Times*, 3 June 1996.
[8] C. Woodroffe, M. Glickham, M. Barker and C. Power, *Children, Teenagers and Health: The Key Data*, Open University Press, 1993.
[9] D. Nicholls and R. Viner, 'Eating Disorders and Weight Problems'. *British Medical Journal*, April 2005.
[10] St Augustine, *Confessions*.
[11] *The Times*, 8 September 1997.

[12] L.J. Francis and W.K. Kray, *Teenage Religion and Values*, Gracewing, 1995.

[13] D. Morris, *The Naked Ape*, Jonathan Cape, 1967.

[14] F. Crick, *The Astonishing Hypothesis: Scientific Search for the Soul*, Simon & Schuster, 1994.

[15] Although others, such as Stephen Jay Gould, thought that 'meme' is a meaningless metaphor.

[16] *The Skeptic*, May 1993.

[17] 'Minds, Memes and Selves', lecture given at the London School of Economics, 28 November 1996.

[18] R. Dawkins, *Climbing Mount Improbable*, Viking, 1996.

[19] 'Why We Exist', public lecture, London, 25 April 1996.

Chapter 5

Just Do It

*Currently, about 6 out of every 100 teenage girls
have an abortion or a baby.*[1]

*The mother of three teenage 'baby factory' sisters has
admitted she gave her blessing to her youngest daughter
having sex when she was just 11.*

DAILY MAIL[2]

'Shut up talking about love – there's no such thing.' This aggressive outburst in one of my school conferences was quite unexpected. At the time I was discussing with the teenagers the teaching of Jesus, one of whose greatest commandments was that we should love one another. One girl obviously couldn't accept this and so she shouted out, 'How can love be so important when it doesn't exist?' I invited her to say more but her eyes then filled with tears and it was clear that she didn't want to.

Later that afternoon the head of the school whispered in my ear some reasons why this girl had such an attitude to love. She had recently been dumped by her boyfriend – as soon as he discovered that she was pregnant. She had subsequently had an abortion and was now suffering from some of the symptoms of what is known as 'post-abortion trauma'. Her hopes and dreams of love had been shattered. Over the space of a few weeks she had changed from a happy, vibrant girl who was enjoying life – to a depressed, cynical girl who no longer believed in the existence of love.

She is one of thousands of teenagers whom I have tried to help overcome the tragedies that their sexual activity has brought into their lives. Some have had abortions, some have had babies, some have picked up sexually transmitted diseases. Many others have avoided all of these obvious dangers, but have found themselves incapable of escaping the unexpected psychological, emotional and spiritual consequences of their sexual activity.

Tina was a virgin when she started at college. She was quite certain that she had worked out her attitude to sex. She had talked it through with her mother and had decided that she would not sleep with any boyfriend unless they had been going out together for six months and she was completely sure that they were in love with each other.

On her first day in the college she noticed a boy that she fancied. They soon started going out together. The relationship developed and she felt sure that they were in love with each other. After six months they slept together. However, in the weeks that followed, their relationship cooled down and they broke up.

Soon afterwards Tina started going out with another boy. The relationship developed and, after just two months, she slept with him. She knew they weren't in love and she knew that she was going back on her decision to wait for six months – but somehow she just couldn't stop herself. Once more the relationship ended. And she started going out with someone else, whom she slept with after just two weeks. The saga continued and she soon found herself going out with a series of different boys and sleeping with them all. It wasn't unusual for her to meet someone at a party and then go straight home to bed with him.

Tina told me that, throughout all this, she hated herself for what she was doing. Each night she would lie in bed thinking, 'What a tart I have become.' But she just didn't seem to be able to stop herself. She didn't have a baby, she managed to avoid all the sexually transmitted diseases, she didn't get AIDS. But, psychologically, emotionally and spiritually, she knew that she was steadily destroying herself.

Tina felt that her heart had been broken through her sexual activity. There are many teenagers like her. But there are many others who are not. They will tell me that they sleep around with lots of different partners and yet they are not broken-hearted. They don't lie in bed at night hating themselves for what they are doing, as Tina did. They say that they are not falling apart because of their sexual promiscuity. Why is this? I find, as I talk more fully with them, that they are clearly telling the truth. But they are only telling part of the truth. They have not become broken-hearted, but they have become hard-hearted.

Trevor was sexually promiscuous and proud of it. He was one of the first of the group of lads he hung out with who managed to go the whole way and sleep with a girl. He wasn't really going out with her. He didn't really care about her. He just wanted to know what it felt like to have sex with a girl. And it felt good. Over the next few years he slept with lots of different girls. With some of them he actually went out with them for some time, and began to form a real relationship with them. But it never seemed to last. He soon felt driven to hunt down another, new, sexual conquest.

Trevor recalled later that, during this time of sexual promiscuity, he seemed to spend as much of his life trying to get rid of a girl that he had slept with as he did trying to find another. In fact, he often didn't even enjoy the sex because, while he was doing it, all he could think about was how he was going to dump the girl afterwards. When he stopped and reflected on his sexual activity, he realised that he didn't really enjoy any of it much anyway. Sure, there was the fun of the chase and there was the thrill of the orgasm. But somehow it all seemed so very empty, so hollow, so unfulfilling.

Trevor didn't feel broken-hearted like Tina did. But, when he allowed himself to think about it, he realised that he did feel hard-hearted. He knew that his sexual promiscuity was taking a toll in his life. He was becoming harder and more lonely in his heart. He never seemed able to become attached to a sexual partner. And he wasn't sure that he ever would be. He seemed to be squeezing out any feelings he had – other than that feeling of cold, raw sex. As he lay in bed at night he didn't feel broken. He didn't feel anything much at all. But he wanted to. He wanted to be warm again. He wanted to be vulnerable, to be intimate, to be romantic, to be passionate.

Both Trevor and Tina were clearly damaged by their sexual activity. The effects were not physical; they were psychological, emotional and spiritual. But they were just as real. And they are all too common.

Research has revealed that 26 per cent of teenage girls and 30 per cent of boys are experiencing sexual intercourse before the age of 16. And not many wait long after that. The average age at first intercourse in the latest National Attitudes and Sexual Lifestyles Survey (Natsal 2000) was 16 years old.[3] This is in marked contrast to the statistics fifty years ago when the average girl was

21 years old before she had sex (and 38 per cent of them were married at the time). Furthermore, most boys do not have sex with a girl because they love her or because they want any kind of ongoing relationship. In fact, only 6 per cent of boys who were sexually active under the age of 16 report that their main motive was love; 40 per cent report that they really did it out of curiosity. Early first intercourse is reported as less likely to be a consensual event, and more likely to be regretted – with less planned protection against pregnancy and infection.[4] Indeed, 10 per cent of boys report that they were under the influence of alcohol or drugs when they first had sex, and 11 per cent of girls felt they were being pressurised into their first experience.[5]

It is inevitable, then, that this leads to problems. Of those girls who first had sex before they were 16 years old, 58 per cent say that they then regretted it. They think that they were too young, and it was too soon for them.[6]

So, why do they do it? Why are so many teenagers sexually promiscuous? There are many reasons. We don't have to look far to see some obvious causes right there on the surface of teenage culture.

The first obvious reason is biological. It has to do with the teenager's hormones. In the pre-teenage years most boys, for instance, are not sexually alert. They view their penis simply as a pipe through which they urinate and they fail to comprehend what pleasure could possibly be derived from the things they learn about in their sex education lessons at school.

But then something happens. Hormones start to flood through their bodies and their sex-drive seems to switch on at full power. Suddenly, they can't even ride on a bus without having a throbbing erection. They become acutely aware of the pleasurable feelings that their penis can give. Their nights are suddenly full of sexually explicit dreams, and they experience their first nocturnal emissions.

What has happened to them? The answer is biological. Their body is now full of hormones. And they feel a physical drive towards expressing and experiencing their sexuality.

The second obvious reason is psychological. It has to do with the teenager's curiosity.

To a young person the world appears a bit like Disneyland. It is full of different opportunities and experiences for them to try. When they are young they enjoy the rides in 'play-world'. Dolls, trains, toy cars and colouring books fill their minds. But then, as they grow into their adolescence, for the first time they notice the signs to 'sex-world'. When they look into this land they see before them huge new rides that they never knew existed. They are full of curiosity. They want to try them out. They want to know what they feel like.

The third obvious reason is sociological. It has to do with their desire to be accepted by those around them.

There is no doubt that teenagers are desperately keen to fit in. They want to be accepted within their peer group. They cannot bear the idea of being stigmatised for being odd or different in any way. So, if others are boasting of their sexual experiences, then they will not want to be left out. It has been said that we live in a culture in which 'no sexual activity is considered deviant – except no sexual activity'. That is, it is acceptable to engage in almost any kind of sex but if you are not sexually active somehow there must be something wrong with you. For some teenagers, therefore, virginity is a stigma to be lost as soon as possible. So, for them, the reason for their sexual behaviour is sociological – they want to fit in.

All three of these reasons are dealt with in detail in

many other excellent books about teenagers. If you want to read more about them there are plenty to choose from. However, as important as these three well-known reasons are, there are other explanations for sexual promiscuity. In particular, there is a more fundamental, philosophical reason why many teenagers, especially, are increasingly promiscuous. This reason does not seem to be covered in books about teenage sexual behaviour. Perhaps it has not yet been recognised or understood by most people. This should give us cause for concern, because this reason is potentially much more damaging to teenagers and our society in general than are any of the other more commonly stated explanations – for it has implications for all sorts of potentially damaging behaviour, not just in the area of sexual promiscuity.

To understand this reason we must, once again, take a step back and think about some of the underlying beliefs that have developed over the centuries, but have only really made it into popular culture in recent years. As we consider these, over the next few pages, we will need to look at some science and some philosophy. Once more, you may wonder what this has got to do with teenage sexual behaviour. But stick with it and all will become clear.

Science and Sex

During the last few centuries people have developed a very high regard for science. Today it seems to provide us with so much. We drive in cars and fly in planes. If we get sick we take antibiotics or fit hip replacements or install pacemakers. It is tempting for us to think, then, that science will give us all the answers to life.

Although science is actually only a methodology (a

way of asking a particular small set of questions about life) there has been a very strong tendency in Western culture to accept it as a philosophy (a belief that these questions are the only ones worth asking). This philosophy is variously described as 'scientism', or 'scientific materialism', or 'naturalism'. For our purposes let's concentrate on the notion of naturalism, and see where this particular philosophy is leading our culture and the teenagers who are growing up within it.

Naturalism is a belief (a statement of faith) that what we can study by means of the natural sciences is really all that there is. According to naturalism there is no need to look beyond or outside the physical world for any supernatural explanations. This rules out any belief in God or a spiritual reality. It even seems to reject the traditional view of a human soul that, in some way, transcends the limits of the physical world.

Nicholas Humphrey, the distinguished theoretical psychologist, put it this way: 'Few adults in the modern world can actually be unaware that there are now physicalist explanations for most if not all natural phenomena, not excluding the workings of the human mind'.[7] Friedrich Nietzsche expressed it in more emotive terms: 'I am body and soul – so speaks the child... But the awakened, the enlightened man says: I am body entirely, and nothing beside; and soul is only a word for something in the body.'[8]

Naturalism has therefore been presented to our culture as a grown-up response to life, which will take us beyond the silly superstitions of the past. It is seen as the logical conclusion of the wonderful science that has brought us so much, and will continue to in the future – if only we will trust it.

Carl Sagan described science as a candle in the darkness which can 'routinely predict a solar eclipse, to the minute, a millennium in advance. You can go to the witch doctor to lift the spell that causes your pernicious anaemia, or you can take Vitamin B12. If you want to save your child from polio, you can pray or you can inoculate. If you're interested in the sex of your unborn child, you can consult plumb-bob danglers all you want . . . but they'll be right, on average, only one time in two. If you want real accuracy try amniocentesis and sonograms. Try science.'[9]

What difference will that make to the sexual behav-iour of young people? Before we can begin to consider this we need to understand two characteristics of beliefs in general.

Firstly, individual beliefs do not stand alone. Each belief carries with it a set of other consequent beliefs. Or, more particularly, it rules out certain other beliefs.

For example, imagine that my son tells me that he doesn't believe in birthdays any more. 'Oh, that's a shame' I reply to him, 'because that means that you won't be getting any cards or presents and you won't have a birthday party.'

'No,' he says, 'I still want those. I still believe in birthday cards, birthday presents and birthday parties. I just don't believe in birthdays anymore.' The fact is that he can't have it both ways. If he no longer believes in birthdays he has automatically ruled out any other beliefs in the things that stem from them. In the same way, if someone decides that they do not believe in the supernatural then they have also automatically ruled out any other beliefs that depend upon the supernatural.

Secondly, any beliefs that we hold tend to have an effect on the way in which we behave. Beliefs even seem to act at an unconscious level. We may not have thought through the implications of a certain belief, nor even be aware that we actually hold that belief at all. And yet the belief does have an effect upon our actions.

Taking these two features of beliefs together, we can see that if we accept one particular belief then it may mean that we have to abandon certain other beliefs and, whether we are aware of it or not, this may have a profound effect upon the way in which we behave.

We will now see how these two features help to explain why naturalism tends to lead to sexual promiscuity. A belief in naturalism rules out a belief in self-control. This is because in order to have self-control we must have free will and, if human beings are nothing but natural physical processes, then free will is one thing that we cannot have. When we lose our belief in the reality of self-control (whether we are consciously aware of it or not), this, in turn, takes the brakes off the biological, psychological and sociological causes that drive us towards sexual activity. Thus it opens the floodgates to sexual promiscuity.

To consider this a bit more slowly let's start with an illustration. Imagine a snooker table with a set of balls upon it. A player walks up to the table, takes his cue in his hand and strikes the white ball. Now suppose that we were able to know every single physical feature about the table. Imagine we know exactly how hard the ball has been struck; in which direction, the precise position of each of the other balls, the friction of the table, the amount of bounce that each cushion provides etc. etc. If we had all that data then it would be possible for us to predict exactly where each of the snooker balls would come to rest.

That is because the snooker table is a purely physical system. The balls have no free will. They don't decide whether they want to move or not. They can't exercise any self-control and decide that they are not going to move once they have been struck. The whole process is determined as if it is controlled by a set of physical laws, which act in a chain of cause and effect – and each effect is completely determined by its cause.

So much for snooker tables. What about the rest of the world? If we believe in naturalism then we find that we must believe that the whole world is like a massive, highly complex snooker table where everything acts in a chain of cause and effect and all events are determined by previously existing natural causes. This logical extension of naturalism is sometimes called 'determinism'.

Pierre Laplace was an eighteenth-century French mathematician and philosopher who was a firm believer in naturalism and determinism. He is best known for the time when he demonstrated to the emperor Napoleon how Isaac Newton's mathematical calculations could explain the irregularities in the movements of planets without the need for a belief in any supernatural adjustment. Napoleon asked him where God fitted in to his ideas. Laplace replied, 'I have no need of that hypothesis.'

Furthermore, Laplace argued that, because everything can be explained naturally and is determined physically, if we were to know the exact position of everything in the entire universe then we would be able to predict everything that would happen throughout the whole universe for the rest of eternity. According to Laplace the whole universe is like that snooker table (but on a much larger scale) where every cause has a predictable effect, so if we know all the causes we can exactly predict all the effects.

But what about human free will? We are part of this universe. Is Laplace saying that it would even be possible to predict every thought, decision and action that humans would make? The answer is: yes. If we accept naturalism then we have to reject the concept of free will. If naturalism means that every part of this world can be explained by natural processes, then that includes human brains. And if every event in this world is determined, then that also includes the events that take place in our brains – our mental processes.

Will Provine, a biologist at Cornell University, has said, 'Humans are comprised only of heredity and environment, both of which are deterministic . . . from my perspective as a naturalist, there's not even a possibility that human beings have free will.'[10]

But what about our personal experience of free will? We don't think that every decision we make is just the effect of a particular set of causes: we experience a sense of freedom. We feel as if we have an ability to choose and to make decisions. But if naturalism is correct then that experience is not real.

The psychologist Susan Blackmore has put it this way: 'The idea that there is a self in there that decides things, acts and is responsible is a whopping great illusion. The self that we construct is just an illusion because actually there is only brains and chemicals and this "self" doesn't exist.'[11]

Similarly, Francis Crick, one of the scientists who unravelled the mystery of DNA, says that our sense of free will is only an illusion. He said that it isn't really true. We may feel as if we have free will, but we don't really because 'your sense of personal identity and free will are in fact no more than the behaviour of a vast assembly of nerve cells and their associated molecules.'[12]

This concept is very hard for people to accept. That is why most people don't think about it. Some, like Susan Blackmore and Francis Crick, have faced up to the implications of their belief in naturalism. Many others have not. They are happy to believe in naturalism, but only because they haven't realised that this necessarily cuts away any belief that they had in free will. Like my son, they want to reject the birthdays but keep the birthday presents.

Incidentally, there is a third set of people who realise the implications of naturalism but try to side-step them with some crafty arguments. They try to say that it is possible to believe in naturalism and yet also believe in free will. They base their argument on the findings of scientists working in the field of quantum mechanics. Such scientists have shown that, although it is true that the world seems deterministic when we look at it on a large scale, when we look at it much more closely we find that it actually appears to be indeterminate. To return to the snooker table illustration, these scientists acknowledge that the movement of the balls seems deterministic but argue that if we were to look inside the balls we would see a different picture.

There is no doubt that when scientists look inside atoms they do see a world that appears random and unpredictable. Albert Einstein argued that this must simply be due to the inadequacy of our current scientific knowledge. He proposed that there must be some hidden variable which, when discovered, will restore determinacy to the whole of physics. However, many scientists don't believe that such a hidden variable exists. Rather, they accept that the subatomic world is actually indeterminate. This has become known as the 'Copenhagen interpretation' because its main promoter, Niels Bohr, worked in that city.

Consequently some people have used this belief in indeterminacy in quantum mechanics in an attempt to believe in both naturalism and free will at the same time. If the subatomic world is not determinate then could this allow us to have free will through purely natural processes? For instance Roger Penrose, the Oxford mathematician, has argued[13] that free will operates at the interface between the subatomic and atomic level in the brain. He has even proposed that it is located in the microtubules which can expand and shrink between the two levels.

However, despite the attempts of Roger Penrose and others, one cannot use such arguments to reconcile naturalism and free will – because the indeterminacy of quantum mechanics is not consistent with free will. Free will is the ability to make a voluntary choice or decision; whereas the indeterminacy in quantum mechanics is due to randomness. This is something quite different. One could try to argue that our decisionmaking processes include elements of randomness along with determinacy. But one cannot argue that this constitutes free will as we understand it and experience it. Randomness is not compatible with voluntary choices or decisions.

Furthermore they would do well to be cautious when they argue that something that seems random is in fact random. Advances in the branch of science known as 'chaos theory' have shown that it is possible for events that appear to be random and chaotic actually to be governed by strictly deterministic laws. The events may not be predictable to us because minute alterations in the cause bring about a great difference in the effect. But they are still deterministic.

So it seems inevitable that those who believe in naturalism must be forced to abandon any belief they might have held in free will. They can (cautiously) replace it with randomness instead of determinacy if they like. But it is still not free will.

It's Not My Fault – Don't Blame Me!

At this point you may be wondering how many of todays

teenagers are aware of such complex scientific and philosophical arguments. And how many, if they did know about them, would understand them anyway? The answer, of course, is: not a lot. But, although they may not have heard of the terms nor understood the concepts, they still seem to have been affected by them. This is because of the way in which they have been taken into popular culture in recent years.

The philosophical belief systems of naturalism and determinism have been known in science for centuries. Throughout that time they seem to have had very little effect upon the average person, and even less upon the average teenager. However, in the last few decades this has all changed.

Today's teenagers are the first generation to have grown up surrounded by such ideas because it is only in the last few decades that naturalism and determinism have been popularised in mainstream culture – largely through the publicity that has been given to the recent research in genetics.

In the middle of the 1980s scientists suggested that they should make a concerted attempt to map the human genome – the total genetic content of a human cell. Thus the Human Genome Project began, based at the new National Centre for Human Genome Research, at the Institute of Health in Bethesda, Maryland. The Congress of the United States allocated some $3,000 million dollars to the project, which officially started on 1 October 1990. The goal was to map the 60,000 to 80,000 human genes in the human genome and to make them accessible for further biological study, as well as to determine the complete sequence of the 3,000 million DNA subunits (bases).

On the one hand the human genome project is simply a scientific investigation. But, on the other hand, it seems to have been used to carry into popular culture the belief that scientists will soon be able to find genes that determine everything about us, including our behaviour.

Consequently, the popular media have been full of stories that researchers have identified genes that determine such behaviour as aggression, crime, depression, alcoholism, or anorexia. Newspapers frequently carry headlines such as 'Scientists identify gene for depression' and 'Aggression is determined by our genes' and 'Official: lust is all in the genes'. The substance is always much less dramatic and conclusive than the headline. But it is the headline that carries the message into popular culture.

As always, there is another side to the story. In the long tradition of the nature-nurture debate, there are those who respond by pointing out that our genes cannot, on their own, determine our behaviour. For instance, when the report entitled 'Genetics of criminal and anti-social behaviour' was published in 1996, Professor Sir Michael Rutter responded by saying, 'Genes do not lead people directly to commit criminal acts. There may be an increased – in some cases greatly increased – propensity to aggression or anti-social behaviour but whether or not the affected individual actually commits some criminal act will also be dependent upon environmental predisposing factors or situational circumstances at the time.'[14]

Similarly Professor Steve Jones responded to the research seeking to identify genes for higher IQ by saying, 'Yes, it may be possible in the future to manipulate those genes. But it would be easier to change a population's IQ by doubling teachers' pay. Social engineering works more effectively. That's why people send their kids to Eton. It's quicker than messing with DNA.'[15]

Notice that, whatever view such scientists express on the nature-nurture debate they still hold to the naturalistic belief in determinism. They may argue that our behaviour is determined by our genes, or by our environment, or by some combination of both. But none of them talks about free will, self-control or individual responsibility. Thus determinism is popularised in mainstream culture. As with the story of the man stealing wheelbarrows which I told in the introduction, there may be heated debate about the content in terms of genes and environment – while the underlying wheelbarrow of determinism gets smuggled through into popular culture unquestioned.

Most teenagers may not be able to define naturalism or determinism, but they have grown up in a world in which those concepts have been popularised. Through this many of them have picked up the idea that their behaviour is, in some way, determined by factors beyond their control.

At a time when they are spreading their wings, thinking for themselves and developing their independence from their parents, today's teenagers are surrounded by a culture that has told them that, somehow, their behaviour is the result of their genes or their environment. We should not, therefore, be surprised when we hear them say, 'Don't blame me,' 'It's not my fault,' or, 'I can't help it.'

If they have absorbed the idea that their behaviour is determined and they have no free will, can we then expect them to take responsibility for their actions, or to exercise self-control? In recent years Western culture has been infused with the implicit assumption that nothing is really anyone's fault, and we are quite powerless to change. We must just go with the flow.

The stand-up comic and writer, Ben Elton has parodied this view brilliantly in his play and novel called *Popcorn*.[16] This is the story of Bruce, a film director, who won't take responsibility for the effect of his films, and Wayne and Scout, two murderers, who won't take responsibility for their crimes.

In a crucial scene, Bruce describes how he got off a drink-driving charge by pleading that he had an addictive personality. He recounts, 'That's what I said. Not "I'm sorry your honour; I'm an irresponsible sh*t," but "I can't help it. I have an addictive personality. I drank the booze, I drove the car but it wasn't my fault." I had a problem you see and it saved me from a prison term.' He then refers to someone else who had been exposed as a serial adulterer. 'He said he was addicted to sex. Not just a gutless, cheating little f**k-rat, you notice. No. A sex addict. He had a problem, so it was not his fault.'

Reflecting on contemporary society, Bruce says, 'Nothing is anybody's fault. We don't do wrong; we have problems. We're victims, alcoholics, sexaholics... Victims!... We are building a culture of gutless, spineless, self-righteous, whining cry-babies who have an excuse for everything and take responsibility for nothing.'

I think Ben Elton has described modern culture very well. The chickens of naturalism and determinism have come home to roost. We have lost our confidence in free will. We have lost our belief in self-control. Consequently, we think we must 'express ourselves' and 'do what comes naturally' and 'be true to ourselves.'

So, if a teenager has had the source of their confidence in self-control taken away, what is there to stop them from giving free rein to the biological, psychological and sociological factors that drive them towards all sorts of sexual activity? The brakes have been taken off and thrown away.

'I just can't stop myself,' said Liz, a 17-year-old who looked strong, capable and self-assured. 'I don't want to sleep around, and when I'm on my own I decide that I'm not going to do it again. But then I go out with a boy, we go back to my room, and I know it's no good trying to stop myself or him. I know I'll hate myself for it afterwards but there's nothing I can do. It happens, it's natural, it's just the way it is.'

Such attitudes should make us very concerned. If the loss of self-control is leading to teenage promiscuity today, then where will it lead tomorrow? Self-control limits not only our sexual activity but also a whole range of other self-destructive and anti-social behaviours.

So how are we going to help teenagers to rediscover their self-control? How can we help them to see that they are not at the mercy of their genes, they are not governed by their glands? How can we enable them to see that they can help it, that they can change?

Here we face another problem. If young people will not accept their own self-control, they are not likely to accept any hint of external control. If they don't think that they have authority in their own life, then they are probably not going to recognise any authority in anyone else either. So, before we turn to possible solutions in Chapter 7, we must consider one last feature of teenage behaviour – their attitude to older people in particular and authority in general.

Notes

[1] C. Woodroffe, M. Glickham, M. Barker and C. Power, *Children, Teenagers and Health: The Key Data*, Open University Press, 1993.

[2] *Daily Mail*, 25 May 2005.

[3] 'Teenage Pregnancy: An Overview of the Research Evidence'. Teenage Pregnancy Unit, Health Development Agency, 2004.

[4] 'Sexual Behaviour in Britain: Early Heterosexual Experience'. K. Wellings et al., *Lancet*, 2001.

[5] 'Sexual Health, Contraception, and Teenage Pregnancy'. J. Tripp

and R. Viner. *British Medical Journal*, March 2005.

6 A. Johnson et al., *Sexual Attitudes and Lifestyles*, Blackwell, 1994.

7 N. Humphries, *Soul Searching*, Chatto & Windus, 1995.

8 F. Nietzsche, *Thus Spake Zarathustra*, translated by R. Hollingdale, Penguin, 1961.

9 C. Sagan, *The Demon-Haunted World – Science as a Candle in the Dark*, Headline, 1997.

10 Recorded in R. Stannard, *Science & Wonders*, Faber & Faber, 1996.

11 *The Skeptic*, May 1993.

12 F. Crick, *The Astonishing Hypothesis: scientific search for the soul*, Simon & Schuster, 1994.

13 See R. Penrose, *The Emperor's New Mind*, Oxford University Press, 1989 and *Shadows of the Mind*, Vintage, 1994.

14 Reported in *The Times*, 24 January 1996.

15 Reported in *The Times*, 12 May 1996.

16 B. Elton, *Popcorn*, Simon & Schuster, 1996.

Chapter 6

Shut Up, Grandad

*25 per cent of school children say that they have
no respect for any teachers.*
DISPATCHES, CHANNEL 4[1]

*46 per cent of 13–15-year-olds say
that they do not find it helpful to talk with their
fathers about their problems.*[2]

Bill was an old man. He was well into his seventies. But his mind was as sharp and clear as ever. He didn't like mysteries; he always wanted to figure them out and understand them. But there was one thing that he found he just could not fathom anymore. That was his 15-year-old grandson.

'I don't know what has happened to John,' he said. 'We used to be so close, but not any more. I remember the time when he seemed to think that I knew everything. If he had a problem he wanted me to fix it. If I told him the best way to do something he immediately believed me. I actually felt a bit embarrassed by the awe and respect in which he held me. But recently things have changed. He seems to think that I know nothing. He doesn't want my advice and certainly won't do anything I tell him. He just makes fun of me and tells me to shut up because I don't understand.'

Bill was worried by John's new attitude to him. Was he right to be so concerned? Is John's attitude really dangerous and disturbing? We might answer both yes and no.

Some of the changes that have taken place in John's attitude to Bill may be considered a normal, healthy part of growing up. As a young boy, John was dependent upon many people, including his grandfather. But he cannot live his whole life in a dependent way – he must become independent. This is clearly vital. All children must learn to stand on their own two feet. It is during the teenage years that they make major steps forward in this progression from dependence to independence.

Such a progression has always happened, as long as human beings have lived on the earth. It has probably always been difficult and painful for children, parents and grandparents alike as they have had to adjust to new relationships and positions.

However, what Bill described was something more than just this transition. John wasn't merely becoming independent of his grandfather, he also seemed to be rejecting him altogether. John didn't just decline his grandfather's advice, he also appeared to ridicule it. He seemed to treat his grandfather as if he knew nothing, as if he were useless. Obviously this worried Bill. I think he was right to be concerned.

As we talked together I tried to help Bill to understand some of the reasons why his grandson may have been behaving in this way, to see the underlying changes that have taken place in the attitude of many teenagers towards older people, and to see this in the context of a wider rejection not just of age in particular, but of all authority.

Let's look at some of the cultural changes that Bill and I discussed. As we have found in the earlier chapters in the book we will need to think quite widely and deeply. Let's start by looking back about 500 years.

Johannes Gutenberg was a fifteenth-century German craftsman who loved to invent things. After spending many years and lots of money he managed to design and build the very first really effective printing press. He could not have realised at that time what an impact this was going to have upon the future of civilisation.

Initially printing was very expensive and, consequently, rather limited. But in time the printing presses of the world began to churn out masses of printed material. Today there are countless millions of books in print, everything from throw-away novels to huge encyclopedias. This has had a profound effect upon the place of elders and tradition in Western culture because the proliferation of printing has moved the main location of knowledge from the human brain to the printed page.

Before Gutenberg's invention, knowledge was mainly held by people. Some things were written down on manuscripts, and laboriously copied for others, but not very many. If you wanted to discover some information you would have to ask someone who knew. For the vast majority of people there were no books that you could read or libraries that you could visit. You had to rely upon the knowledge held by others.

In most cases the people who held the knowledge were older people. They had lived the longest and so had been able to accumulate the most information. They had learned it from their elders, who in turn had received it from their elders – and they knew that this chain went back in time through a rich family and tribal tradition that was highly respected.

It is not surprising, then, that older people were held in very high regard. They were crucial for the development of younger people. And the traditions through which younger people learned from older people were vital to the survival of the culture. This meant that history was very important to everyone, both young and old. They knew that they were not the only generation that had ever mattered. They were dependent on their elders and their traditions. Their heritage was vitally important to them.

There are some parts of the world today where this still applies. There are cultures which we sometimes (rather patronisingly) call primitive and which have no printed, or perhaps even written, material. In these communities knowledge is still held by older people. It is significant that, in such cultures, ancestors, living elders and tribal traditions are still held in high regard. They are vital to the storage and transmission of knowledge and the survival of the culture.

However, printing tends to change this. The printing press makes knowledge available to everyone, regardless of their relationship to older people or their experience of tribal traditions. In the West, for instance, we are surrounded by books. There are libraries full of them. Many people have scores, if not hundreds, of them in their own home. So, if people want to find out some information they can look it up in a book or read it in a newspaper or a magazine. They no longer need an older person.

Similarly, our education system centres around books and not around elders and traditions. Our young people do not learn through sitting around the campfire listening to old people telling the traditional tribal stories. They learn at school, using books. Thus, old people (and particularly old family members) are removed from the educational process. And so it is not surprising that old people are no longer held in very high regard.

But why is it that the effects of this change seem to have become apparent only in recent years? If the printing press was invented 500 years ago why have the consequences taken so long? Clearly there are other factors at work here.

To some extent, it seems that the printing press effect was delayed until widespread schooling developed. It is only in the twentieth century that all young people have received a long, book-based education. Previously, despite the existence of the printing press, many young people still learned a trade through a period of apprenticeship to older people.

To a greater extent, the printing press effect seems to have been increased in the second half of the twentieth century, as it was multiplied by a growth in the amount of knowledge available. Take the world of science, for example, and consider how much has been discovered in the last fifty years. Thus any knowledge that an older person holds seems ever smaller compared to the total knowledge available in books. Furthermore, the knowledge they do have may now be out of date. Grandad may have learned about Newton's laws of physics, but how much does he know about cryogenics, the anthropic principle or artificial intelligence?

But those two factors do not explain the great changes in the recent decades. Another new factor must be added to the printing press effect – the invention of personal computers and the Internet.

The printing press moved the location of knowledge from the elder's brains to the book. But books were equally accessible to old and young alike. The technological revolution of recent decades has taken knowledge on to computers – which tend to be less accessible to many older people.

Computers have opened up possibilities for information storage and retrieval that could not have been imagined a generation ago. I myself have a copy of the *Encyclopaedia Britannica* on a single CD-ROM, and another CD that contains the text of over 3,500 of the world's classic literary works, from Hippocrates, through William Shakespeare to Mark Twain.

In turn, computers have opened the door to the Internet. For a few pounds each month, it is possible to access information from computers right across the world. Whatever your area of interest you can obtain apparently limitless amounts of knowledge at the press of a button or the click of a mouse.

Today's teenagers are the first generation to have grown up surrounded by such technology. Many of them spend large amounts of time with their fingers on a keyboard and their eyes on a screen. For this reason, Douglas Rushkoff[3] has given a new name to these teenagers: he calls them 'screenagers'.

Thus, while teenagers are able to access this newly available wealth of knowledge, many elderly people are not. Computer skills are picked up quite easily by teenagers, and even by those much younger. But older people typically find it much harder. Many elderly people don't want to touch a computer at all.

Is this the reason why many teenagers seem to regard older people as an embarrassing irrelevance, well past their sell-by date? It clearly explains a lot. But there are also some other issues we need to consider.

Knowledge or Wisdom?

The rejection of older people through the development of printing, computers and the Internet has been possible only because knowledge has been much more highly valued than wisdom. If we are to find a solution to the problem of many teenagers' views of older people it is vital that we understand the difference between these two concepts.

'Knowledge' can be defined as a body of truth or information that has been acquired. These facts or data can be held by a person or in a book or on a computer. Wisdom is quite different. This is the ability to discern; it involves inner qualities and good sense. It cannot be contained in a book or on a computer, but only in a person.

It is true that there are books that we might be tempted to think contain wisdom – such as the ancient Egyptian *Instruction of Amenemope*, some of the Mesopotamian writings, and the book of Proverbs in the Bible. However, despite the fact that these are often called 'wisdom literature', they are not wisdom. They are wise sayings. Even if one had a library full of such wise sayings, or logged on to a database on which they were all indexed, one would not have wisdom. The essential characteristic of wisdom is the ability to discern. This cannot be written down or encoded on a computer disc. Wisdom is not a piece of abstract information; it is a feature of a human being. One cannot *have* wisdom, in the sense that one can have a set of information or a piece of knowledge; one is wise.

Wisdom, then, is hard to attain. It takes time. It cannot be accessed immediately or downloaded from a Web site. In recent years, with the phenomenal growth of knowledge, and the desire for immediate, instant access, it is not surprising that our culture has come to value knowledge above wisdom.

Some saw this coming. The great Martin Luther King put it this way: 'Our scientific power has outrun our spiritual power. We have guided missiles and misguided men.' Similarly, Winston Churchill said, 'We know how to control everything except man himself.'

Many teenagers today also recognise an emptiness in knowledge without wisdom. They have found that, no matter how much they learn at school or college, this doesn't seem to help them with the big issues of life. I remember one biology student putting this very clearly when he said, 'My course tells me how I live – but not what I should live for.' If we can help teenagers to find this wisdom then perhaps they would have answers to their big questions. And also, almost as a by-product, they would once more see the immense value in older people.

But wisdom brings with it authority. So, if they are to find wisdom, they must be prepared to accept authority. And here we face another problem.

In recent years many teenagers have not only rejected older people in particular, but also authority in general. Teachers are not usually respected simply because they are teachers. They need to work very hard to earn the respect that they once had by right. The police have a similar problem.

So why are we facing this crisis of authority? Why do so many teenagers seem to reject any form of authority? To understand this we need to look at some etymology[4] as well as some political history and philosophy.

The word 'authority' is derived from the word 'author'. Thus, in the original meaning of the term, the concept of authority derived from the concept of an author. If an author has created something, she necessarily has rights over that which owes its very existence to her – she has authority over it. She may give that authority to someone else, but that authority is only worth anything because it comes from her, the creator.

If we look back in history, we find that civilisations have always derived their concept of authority from a belief in a creator God. That God is the ultimate author, and therefore the ultimate source of all authority. God may then give individual authority to people on earth – whether grandparents or parents, teachers or kings – but that authority is only worth anything because it comes from the creator.

For example, in ancient China rulers were thought to have the *'T'ien Ming'* – the mandate of heaven. This Chinese Confucian idea had its beginnings in the early Chou dynasty, about 1000BC. The Chinese believed that heaven gave the right to rule directly to an emperor, who was seen as the Son of Heaven.

Many centuries later, in the Byzantine Empire around the eastern Mediterranean, the concept known as 'caesaropapism' was developed. This was a system whereby the emperor was recognised as the head of both the church and the state. The Byzantines believed that, in both these roles, he derived his authority from God.

The idea was later formulated into the belief in the 'divine right of kings', by people such as the French bishop Jacques Bossuet and the English squire Sir Robert Filmer. The divine right of kings was based upon the view that kings derive their authority directly from God. Unfortunately, it was also extended to the belief that, because of the source of their authority, they could not be held accountable for their actions to any earthly authority – such as a parliament. Of course this led to abuses. Therefore it was rejected by philosophers such as John Locke (with his *First Treatise of Civil Government* in 1689). And it was fought against in the English Civil War, the French Revolution and the American War of Independence.

However, these struggles were not fought against the concept of a creator God who gives authority but against the regal misuse of that concept. For instance, the classic rejection of the authority of kings, the American Declaration of Independence, says that governments 'derive their just power from the consent of the governed' but that this, in turn, comes from the fact that 'they are endowed by their Creator with certain unalienable rights'. So, even though the king's authority was rejected, the people still believed that authority is ultimately derived from God.

In the years since then, however, God himself has been largely rejected by Western culture, as we have seen in earlier chapters of this book. But if a culture has declared that God is dead, what then happens to authority? If a belief in authority is derived from a belief in an author, what happens when people no longer believe that there is an author?

The French atheistic philosopher, Jean-Paul Sartre, gave a clear answer to these questions in his famous lecture, entitled 'Existentialism and Humanism', which he delivered in Paris in 1944. In this he said, 'God does not exist and we have to face all the consequences of this . . . it is extremely embarrassing that God does not exist, for there disappears with him all possibility of finding values in an intelligible heaven . . . we find no values or commands to turn to.'

Quite right. If there is no God, then there is no ultimate author and so there is no ultimate authority. We must make up our own mind about right and wrong, truth and error. Thus, there are no absolutes; everything depends upon the individual. Individuals may join together and make a 'social contract' on the basis of an agreed consensus but this may be different for different peoples at different times – so there is still no ultimate basis for authority.

This position is usually referred to as 'relativism'. Relativism says that there is no absolute truth, and no absolute right or wrong. Everything depends upon who you are, where you are, what you are, when you are.

Relativism was perhaps most clearly expressed by the Cambridge scholar Don Cupitt: 'Capital T truth is dead ... Truth is plural, socially conditioned and perpetually changing.' It is more commonly revealed in statements such as 'That's OK for you but it is not true for me.'

Once again, today's teenagers are the first generation to have grown up in a culture that is steeped in relativism. Within a few decades of Sartre's lecture we find that most teenagers seem to agree with him. This is so even among church-attending teenagers. A survey of 677 teenagers who attend church found that only 21 per cent of them believe that there is such a thing as absolute truth.[5]

This loss of absolute truth and absolute right and wrong is bound to have consequences for society. Sartre, in his lecture, quoted the Russian novelist Dostoievsky, who had said, 'Everything is permissible if God does not exist.' Correct. If there is no God, then we cannot really talk about anything being wrong. Nothing can be absolutely wrong. It is just wrong for us, in our culture, at our time, if we decide it is wrong.

I work with teenagers day by day, helping them to explore spiritual and moral issues. Until a few years ago I had never met a completely relativist teenager. When they thought about it they all believed that some things were absolutely wrong. If I asked them whether rape or child abuse is wrong they would tell me, 'Of course it is.' They believed these are wrong not just because we choose to say that they are, but because they are. They didn't always know why, but they believed these things are absolutely wrong.

However, in my experience, this has begun to change in the past few years. I now meet increasing numbers of teenagers who are quite convinced that nothing is absolutely wrong. Just a few days before writing this I led a school conference for 120 teenagers, of whom about ten argued very vigorously with me that nothing, even child abuse or rape, is absolutely wrong. 'Morality,' they said, 'is decided by consensus. Things are only right or wrong if we decide that they are – so nothing can be absolutely wrong.'

This may shock us. But it should not be surprising. If our culture has rejected God, is it not inevitable that people will reject authority? If there is no God to give any ultimate authority, if everything is relative and we must all make up our own minds, why should anyone accept anyone else's authority?

You may decide that something is right, but I may have a different view. Who is to say that you are right and I am wrong? So what if you happen to be a policeman, a teacher, or a judge – or even any older person? Why is your view any better than mine, just because you are older, or hold a particular position? Why should you have any authority over me?

There is a tendency among today's teenagers to lose their concept of authority along with their appreciation of the value of wisdom, their family, national heritage and older people.

Such a conclusion may lead us to think that those of us who are older will never be able to relate properly to teenagers, let alone help them. Even if we have understood all the reasons underlying each aspect of the behaviour that we have considered in this book it would seem that there is nothing that we can do about it – because they are not going to listen to us anyway.

It is clearly true that we cannot just tell them what to

do. But are there ways in which we can help them – as individuals and as a society? I believe there are – as we will see in the final chapter.

Notes

1 Survey by Exeter University for the Channel 4 programme *Dispatches*, 1996.
2 L.J. Francis and W.K. Kray, *Teenage Religion and Values*, Gracewing, 1995.
3 D. Rushkoff, *Children of Chaos (Surviving the End of the World as We Know It)*, HarperCollins, 1997.
4 'Etymology' is the study of the development of words through history.
5 Survey by the Christian Research Association, published in their journal *Quadrant*, Autumn 1997.

Chapter 7

What You Gonna Do About It?

I believe that this final chapter is the most important one in the book. At present you may not agree. You may think that this chapter is unnecessary. If you have read the book because you wanted some basic help to enable you to relate better to your teenage child or nephew or pupil, you may have found that you already have all the help you need. It is possible that, as you have read through the first six chapters, you have already worked out what you are going to do. It may be that, as you have gained more insight into why teenagers behave the way they do, you have realised for yourself what you need to do.

I have seen this reaction many times, with parents in particular. So often they have come to me asking for specific advice about how they should handle a particular situation involving an individual teenager. But then we find that such specific advice is not actually necessary. Once I have helped them to understand why their teenager is behaving as they are, they then tell me that they now realise what they must do – and they clearly don't need any advice from me. Perhaps that's the way it is with you right now, and you are tempted to put the book away. But please don't do so yet.

There is also a sense in which this final chapter cannot be written. Each situation is different, so how can anyone provide any worthwhile, specific advice? When people come to me for help I always begin by listening to their story. Not surprisingly, each story is different from any other story I have heard before. We don't have identical lives. There are so many different factors and we all have so many different experiences. It would simply not be possible for me (or anyone else) to give complete, universal prescriptions which could be written in a chapter like this and applied by everybody in whatever situation they find themselves.

But I can give some general advice which I hope will be helpful. Each reader will need to weigh this up in relation to their own situation and apply, modify or reject it as appropriate. I will look back at the underlying issues that we have discovered and suggest a few general ways in which we might use that information to enable us to help today's teenagers. You may find different parts of this general advice more or less helpful, according to the individual situation you face with any particular teenager you are trying to help.

However, this final chapter simply must be written, and I believe that it is the most important one in the book – not for today's teenagers but for tomorrow's. Teenagers are not going to die out with this generation. No matter how able (or unable) we are to help today's teenagers, we must recognise that there will be another generation of teenagers to come, and then another and another. If the culture in which we currently live has led to problems for today's teenager, then we must try to change it – for the sake of the next generation. In the introduction I quoted from the writings of the American social commentator Douglas Rushkoff. When Rushkoff looks at the massive changes that have taken place in Western culture he says,

'Without having migrated an inch we have nonetheless travelled further than any generation in history.'[1] He goes on to liken us to new immigrants in a new land: we are puzzled and perplexed by the strange world around us. He then argues that, if we are to settle into this new land, we must do what immigrants usually do – that is, follow our children. Since immigrants' children always lead the way in adapting to their new home, he argues that we should follow the attitudes, beliefs and values of today's 'children of chaos'. He says, 'Chaos is their natural environment. By following our screenagers' example rather than panicking at their embrace of turbulence, we may just stand a chance of adapting to the culture to which we are inevitably migrating.'

Is this correct? I find myself agreeing with his analysis but disagreeing with his prescription. For there is another way of looking at the situation we face. Suppose I am an immigrant in a new land, and I see my children adapting to their new home in ways that are deeply damaging to them and to others. What would I do? Rather than following their lead in settling down, I would try to change the land so that it will not harm the children of future generations.

That, I believe, is the situation we currently face in Western culture. Day by day I look at teenagers who are being profoundly damaged by the new world in which they live. And so I want to see that culture changed – for the teenagers of tomorrow. Therefore, in this chapter, as well as suggesting ways in which we may help today's teenagers I also want to consider a fundamental cultural change which I believe is vital for the sake of tomorrow's teenagers. That's why I think this chapter is so important. It is no good us simply going along with the culture or wringing our hands in despair. We must pull up our sleeves and try to change things.

Helping Today's Teenagers

When Luke and Lizzie, my children, were young they enjoyed playing in the snow. They particularly enjoyed sledging. On one occasion they were sat on the sledge at the top of the steepest, fastest slope in the middle of our snow-covered local park. They pushed off and soon gathered speed. I wasn't sure whether they were being brave or foolhardy – because this particular slope had a water-filled ditch at the end of it, and they were not very good at steering. In fact as the sledge picked up speed it became clear that they had very little control over it at all. But they did have an implicit faith in me, whom they had asked to stand in front of the ditch to stop them falling in.

So there I was with this heavy sledge coming straight towards me at high speed. There was no way I would be able to stop it. If I tried I would get hurt and so would they – and we would probably all end up in the water. So I stood aside. I moved out of the way. And as the sledge carrying my children went past me I ran alongside them and gently nudged it. That was enough to change its direction. It turned to the left, on to another slope that took it away from the ditch. So they didn't end up in the water. They were safe. I was unharmed. And they were delighted with their extra-long ride.

That is a picture of the task that faces many of us as we try to help today's teenagers. We watch them as they gather speed downhill on a course that will inevitably hurt them and others. If we try to stand in their way they will collide with us in a huge confrontation. But, if we run alongside and gently nudge them in another direction, we might be able to help them to find another path.

How to be Positively Critical

In chapter one we saw how teenagers have learned to criticise, through the educational shift from the didactic to the critical method, and then how many have become cynical, through the philosophical shift from modernism to postmodernism. How are we best to respond to this?

When teenagers are critical, many of us find that we become defensive – or even offensive. Perhaps we want to defend the object of the criticism or to attack the teenager for their attitude. Thus we may respond in a hostile way. For instance, when a teenager looks at something and says, 'That's a load of rubbish' (or other equivalent but more colourful words), we may become defensive and say, 'No it's not; it's perfectly alright!' Or we might go on the offensive and say, 'Why do you always have to criticise everything!'

Both of these responses are the verbal equivalent of trying to stand in front of the sledge. If we are strong enough, we might be able to stop the teenager – but we are more likely to find ourselves flattened. This may then hurt them or us. Either way, it will damage the relationship between us. So, in the same way that it was possible to deflect the sledge on to a less harmful route, is there a way in which we could deflect the teenager? Can we stand aside and gently nudge them so that they can find another path? I believe that we can.

If you cast your mind back to Chapter 1, you will recall that the problem for teenagers is not so much with the critical method as a methodology (a way of finding answers in the world) but rather with the effect that postmodernism has upon the critical method, in that it tends to lead to a cynical conclusion (a belief that there are no answers to find). Thus, the 'steep slope' of the critical method becomes a problem because it leads into the 'water-filled ditch' of the postmodern conclusion. Perhaps, then, the way forward is to run alongside today's teenagers, helping them to continue questioning along new avenues and new routes – without giving up and coming to cynical conclusions.

When a teenager says, 'That's a load of rubbish,' they may appear to be stating a view. It sounds like a cynical conclusion at which they have arrived. But all may not be lost; it may be possible to develop this statement as a way of questioning about the world. If we were to take time to be with them and to gently reply with a question such as, 'Why do you think it is rubbish?' then we may be able to help them to keep on questioning and thinking. More important than that, we will be with them, running alongside them, helping them to question and thus developing our relationship rather than breaking it apart.

This approach means spending more time listening to teenagers than talking to them. It means making it quite clear that we value their opinions and want to help them to think things through and to search for truth. It means joining with them in their search, being alongside them in their questioning.

You may recall Andy, the character in Chapter 1 who said, 'What's the point . . . it's all rubbish, there's no point.' When I sat with him on the floor and made it clear that I really wanted to listen to him, he gradually (very gradually, in fact) began to talk. As he saw that I wasn't going to knock down the things he said, but rather was willing to investigate them more fully, he steadily developed the confidence to express himself more clearly. Over time he began to see that it was worth searching, thinking and questioning. Perhaps there was a truth to find. When the time came for me to leave he didn't want to stop. He was no longer in the ditch – he was back on the slope.

Helping Andy was a bit like helping my wife, Carol, to buy clothes in a shop. When she comes out of the changing room with a dress on, Carol will have been very careful to make sure that it is all done up properly. It may look as if she is going to wear it as her dress from now on – that is, it may seem that she has come to a conclusion. But really she is just trying it on to see if it fits – and she wants me to join with her in asking questions about it. In the same way, often teenagers may seem to have adopted a particular view – they may even state it in very dogmatic terms. But they may be simply trying the view on for size, to see if it fits. So they can be encouraged to keep on questioning it, and to build their relationship with us in the process.

This doesn't mean that we don't ever want them to come to conclusions. Of course we do. Eventually Carol needs to choose a dress. It may take a long time (sometimes a very, very long time) but she will have to come to a conclusion eventually. We can't live completely on questions; we can't live totally in doubt. Someone has said that doubt is a bit like the Channel Tunnel: it is a great way of getting to the other side, but you wouldn't want to live in it.

This is one of the problems that the shift into postmodernism has produced. Postmodernists tell us that there are really no answers to find. Thus, today's teenagers are implicitly encouraged to take things apart. But they are not told what to do with the bits; in fact they are told that there is not really anything they can do with them anyway.

I believe that, for the sake of tomorrow's teenagers, we must try to move our culture through postmodernism to a philosophy that is built upon more solid and secure foundations. We cannot stay with postmodernism. It will not last; it is self-defeating. In its very nature it does not claim to be an answer. It is a denial of answers. It is a philosophy that essentially defines itself not in terms of what it is, but of what it is not: it is not modern, it is post-modern.

Since postmodernism denies answers and even denies rationality, we cannot just shrug our shoulders and say, 'That's the way the world is now'. For the sake of future generations we must return to a search for answers and to a confidence in rationality.

But here lies a major problem. Can we have confidence in rationality? In the days when our culture believed that human beings were created in the image of God we had good reason to have confidence in our rational nature. If God is rational, then so are we: we can trust our brains because God made them. However, if there is no God, if we have simply evolved by chance, there is no reason why our brains should actually be trusted to reason reliably at anything above a very basic level.

Darwin himself recognised this problem. From an evolutionary point of view, one would expect human thinking to be reliable enough to collect food, to mate, to rear young ones and to control a few other basic activities without which we would not survive. But why should the brain be reliable at any levels of thinking higher than that?

It seems that, for us to be truly confident in rationality, we need to think again about our culture's rejection of God.

We saw in Chapter 1 that, after the Enlightenment, Western culture assumed that we do not need God – we can find the answers to life's problems on our own. However, this Enlightenment optimism did not bear fruit. We did not find satisfactory and sufficient answers. So we then assumed that there are no answers to find.

But there is another possibility. Perhaps there are

satisfactory and sufficient answers to life but they can only be found through the person who created it in the first place.

I am not suggesting, for one moment, that we should go back to pre-modernism which was based upon man-centred church dogma. We must not lose the positive insights of the Enlightenment, about the value of facts and rationality and truth expressed through testable propositions. Similarly, we must not lose the positive insights of postmodernism, about the value of feelings and experience and truth expressed through narrative stories.

Rather, I am suggesting that we should consider whether it is possible to move forward beyond modernism and postmodernism to some kind of holistic culture which recognises humans as physical, mental and spiritual beings designed and equipped to live in relationship with the world, with one another, and with God, who created and sustains it all. If God exists then he will be the source of all facts, the reason for our rationality, the basis of our feelings, the ground of our experience. Perhaps God would also bring his truth to us both in testable propositions and narrative stories.

If it were possible to rediscover God in our culture we would then also find a new model for education – because we would have found a new understanding of the nature of knowledge. The didactic model was based upon a dogmatic view of knowledge, as something that the teacher holds and communicates to the pupil. The critical method is based on a relativistic view of knowledge, as something which pupils construct for themselves. However, if we recognised God as the creator and the source of all knowledge, then we would be able to construct a new model for education, through which the teacher and the pupil work together to seek the knowledge which is accessible to us in the physical realm (through the sciences), in the mental realm (through the humanities) and in the spiritual realm (through theology).

Such a rediscovery of God may also open up new ways for us to handle the otherwise seemingly insurmountable problem of teenage drug abuse which we face today.

Dealing with the Boredom and Searching for a Community

We saw in Chapter 2 how many teenagers take drugs to deal with their sense of boredom and to become part of a community that is experiencing something beyond the mundane material world. How, then, are we to help them?

I believe that we must begin by acknowledging exactly what it is that teenagers have discovered. Despite the constant pressure of this fast-paced, high-tech, multi-media world, they have found that it cannot provide the excitement they seek and expect. So they are looking for other ways to fulfilment. Their solution is to try drugs, because these appear to provide what they want. At its heart, the problem is not that they are looking for fulfillment but that they are looking in a dangerous place. If that is so, then we must help them to look elsewhere.

It would clearly be a mistake to try to push them back into looking for fulfilment in the fast-paced, high-tech, multimedia world. Again this is like trying to stop the sledge. And yet that is what we may be tempted to do. Perhaps we mistakenly think that if teenagers are getting bored with something then the answer is to make it more exciting.

Thus those of us who lead Scout groups or run youth

clubs might think that, in order to attract and keep teenagers, we must make our events as fast and loud as the adverts and the MTV. Similarly parents try to think of exciting places to take their teenagers on holiday. And yet, if we do this, we will then face the same problem as the advertisers and TV producers. We will keep moving the goal-posts and we will continually need to find an activity even more exciting than last week's, or a holiday destination even more exciting than last year's.

Is it not better, then, to help them to keep looking – but to gently nudge them to look elsewhere for fulfilment? But where can we help them to look? Perhaps they already have the answer in the fact that they want to be part of a community that is experiencing something beyond the physical world.

Once again we are driven to the possibility that the answer may be found in the God whom this culture has chosen to reject. If God exists, then might it be possible to find in him a spiritual fulfilment far better than the dead-end excitement of the modern world, or the chemical buzz of heroin? And might it be possible to be part of a spiritual community that is experiencing something beyond this mundane physical world but isn't dependent upon the effects of ecstasy?

Cathy was a teenager who wanted to be a lighting engineer. In her college she had learned how to run the small, permanent lighting rig in the college hall, and we booked her to run the lights for a Friday night concert by a young band who had been working with me in a series of events at her college. In the middle of that concert I was invited on stage to talk about my experience of God. At the time I didn't realise how intently she was listening, in the privacy of the lighting booth. But afterwards she came up to me, in tears, and poured out her heart. She told me how, for some time, she had been using drink and drugs, but how those substances now seemed to be using her – and she wanted to find another way.

After a long conversation we prayed together and she cried out to God, not even really sure if he existed, asking him to show her another way. Some months later she came on one of the residential weekend retreats which I ran for teenagers in her area. Joining with about a hundred other teenagers, she experienced what it meant to be part of a drug-free community who were seeking spiritual fulfilment in God.

She began to see that fulfilment did not necessarily mean excitement. She began to discover the joy of prayer, and the pleasure of peacefulness. She also found that there was an excitement in knowing God, and a buzz from worshipping him with others. But this was an excitement and a buzz that delivered what they promised.

Sometime after this I talked to her and asked her how her life was going. She told me how, through these events, she had become a Christian, had joined a church and wanted to experience more of God in her life. However, she also told me that her parents were not at all happy with this and had done everything they could to turn her away from God and the church. She recounted how her dad had said to her, 'I preferred it when you were into drink and drugs, rather than all this stuff about God.'

I think her parents had made a big mistake and I urge others not to do the same. Should we not actively help teenagers to explore the possibility that the fulfilment in life that they seek may be found in a spiritual rather than a chemical reality? If that is so, might it also be possible that God may provide a way for us to deal with the pain in our lives as well?

Dealing with the Pain

In Chapter 3, we considered how we now live in an anaesthetic age and in a sanitised society. When teenagers experience emotional pain they tend to view it as something that should not be there and so must be removed by drugs or even suicide.

However, it is possible to view pain in another way – as an experience that may bring us to a new understanding of life.

Jess is a young woman who works with me occasionally when I speak at universities. When she was a teenager herself she was looking forward to a career on the stage as an actress, singer and dancer. One night she went out to a nightclub with some friends. They had more to drink than they had intended and decided it wasn't safe to drive home. Instead they went to sleep in the car.

However, in the middle of the night the driver woke up, decided that he was now sober, and thought he would surprise everyone by driving them home while they slept. Unfortunately, he wasn't fit to drive, and he crashed the car. Most of the passengers got away with short-term injuries but Jess was flung out of the door and broke her back.

When she regained consciousness and realised that she was paralyzed, Jess became aware that she had a choice to make. She could cry out to God in anger and hatred, or she could cry out for help. Whichever way she cried she knew that she would have to wrestle with the question of why had this happened to her, but the 'why?' of a seeking hand is very different from the 'why?' of a clenched fist.

Jayne works with me regularly as part of my team running school conferences. Not many years ago, when she was a teenager herself, Jayne was engaged to be married to a boy named David. They bought a flat, settled down and had great plans for their new life together. But then David became ill with a rare heart-lung disorder for which there was no cure. During the months that followed, Jayne watched the health of her young husband steadily deteriorate, until she nursed him through his death. As she struggled with this terrible experience, Jayne, also, knew that she could either turn to God or away from him.

Both Jayne and Jess lived with the pain, and still do. Both of them say that, while they didn't want the pain, they know that it has had a transforming effect upon them. Jayne has said on many occasions, 'People seem to think that suffering proves that there is no God. All I can say is that my suffering proved to me that God is real – as he came to be with me in it.' Similarly, Jess has known a transformation in her life and in the lives of others around her as she has been enabled to live through the pain.

Somehow, we have to help other teenagers to cope with the pain that they will inevitably face in their lives. We must help them to see it not as an experience from which they must run away, but as one they can live through and grow through, as Jess and Jayne both did. How can we do that?

First of all, we must unsanitise society. It is a great mistake to give young people the impression that they can go through life without experiencing pain and sickness – whether physical or emotional. I believe that we should take our children to hospital; we should help them to develop friendships with old, sick and dying people. We should encourage them to see dead bodies and to mourn with those who mourn. They need to see that sickness and death is not just something that happens on the TV and in films, as if it were just some fictional concept, but rather it is something which we all must face together as human beings.

Secondly we must unanaesthetise our society. We must learn that pain cannot always be taken away. We cannot run away from it. We have to learn to deal with it.

But, most of all, we must help teenagers to see that pain and death can be a source of transformation. Every teenager is different and there will be no set way to help them to learn this lesson. But in my experience a very good way forward is through taking opportunities to let teenagers hear of others who have found pain to be a transforming experience. We can use some of the great stories of history and literature. There are many examples of the transforming power of pain and suffering, from the diary of Anne Frank to C.S. Lewis' lion called Aslan. Or the lesson may be imparted through contemporary real-life stories, such as those of Jess and Jayne – as I have seen many times when they told their stories to teenagers; or through the greatest story of the transforming power of suffering – the crucifixion of Jesus.

There was a time when every teenager in our culture knew the biblical story of Jesus' death on the cross. Today, however, many teenagers are unfamiliar with this. A 1991 MORI poll revealed that 57 per cent of 18-year-olds don't know what event took place on Good Friday.[2] And many who know the story fail to see its significance or relevance for their lives.

A good way forward for those of us seeking to help teenagers who feel a sense of hopelessness and despair from the pain in their lives is to help them to consider and understand the message of Jesus' death and resurrection – with all that it teaches us about forgiveness, hope and about new life.

If we can help them to do this, then we might also be able to help them to think again about our own value, and that of other people (especially older people). To think about whom we should want to worship, and whom we should strive to follow. To consider whether we are free to exercise self-control, whether we can be held accountable for our actions and whether there is any ultimate authority in the world. We looked at these issues in Chapters 4, 5 and 6 – and I will now consider them together.

Value, Freedom and Authority

In Chapter 4 we noted that we all seem to have an in-built desire to worship and follow someone or something greater than ourselves. For centuries people in the West worshipped God and aspired to follow him, thus seeking to change their character and inner nature. In recent years, however, as God has been rejected, people have worshipped pop stars, sportsmen and supermodels – and have aspired to follow them, thus seeking to change their image and external nature.

So, faced with that problem, how can we help today's teenagers to value internal character rather than external appearance? We might think that the answer lies in education: perhaps we should ask the schools to teach about the value of internal character rather than scholastic attainment. Or we might think that the answer lies in the home: perhaps we should teach parents how to reward and develop good character rather than good skills, gifts and abilities. Or we might think the answer lies with the media: perhaps we should encourage films and TV programmes that celebrate internal character rather than external appearance. Or we might think the answer lies in the fashion industry: perhaps we should encourage the modelling of good character instead of good figures.

All these practical approaches may be valuable for today's teenagers. However, each of these explicit attempts to teach the value of internal character will find itself struggling uphill against the powerful implicit message that internal character is not so important. This message derives from the fact that the culture tells us the nihilistic message that we are accidentally evolved bundles of chemicals and neurones with no ultimate value other than that which we choose to ascribe to ourselves. If we are concerned for tomorrow's teenagers we must deal with this.

In Chapter 5, we saw how naturalism and determinism lead many teenagers to assume implicitly that they are somehow at the mercy of their genes or their environment. Thus, many of them have lost confidence in the concept of self-control.

How are we going to help today's teenagers to rediscover this? Once again we could say that the answer lies in education, the home, or the media. We could look for ways to teach and encourage self-control. We could find ways to give teenagers more responsibility and hold them accountable for how they exercise it. We could seek to encourage teenagers to read books or watch films that highlight the value of honour, patience and self-control. We could find ways to encourage them to go on Outward Bound courses or work for the Duke of Edinburgh Award, where they will learn that they can control their bodies, that they don't have to give up and take the easy route.

All of these practical attempts to help today's teenagers to discover that they can exercise self-control, that they can be responsible, that they are not at the mercy of deterministic factors, may be helpful. But, once again, they will struggle uphill against the powerful implicit message of naturalism that tells us that our behaviour is determined by our genes and our environment. If we are concerned for tomorrow's teenagers we must deal with this.

In Chapter 6 we saw how older people have become marginalised because of the way in which our culture prizes knowledge above wisdom; and we saw how we have lost confidence in the notion of authority because of our rejection of the concept of an author, and the consequent relativisation of truth and morals.

So how are we going to help today's teenagers to deal with this? Yet again we could say that the answer lies in education, the home, or the media. We could look for ways to teach our teenagers about the value of older people. We could find older people with skills and abilities that our teenagers need (such as the ability to fix their car or improve their football skills) and put them together. We could find old people with interesting personal stories to tell, whom our teenagers could interview for their history projects. We could organise or enter pub competitions that require older and younger people to pool their knowledge to succeed. We could ask our teenagers to use their computer to draw up and record the family tree.

All of these practical attempts to help today's teenagers to discover the value of their heritage and their place in history may be helpful. But they will struggle uphill against the powerful implicit message that stems from the rejection of wisdom and authority, and the consequent moral relativism. If we are concerned for tomorrow's teenagers we must deal with this.

Getting to the Heart of the Problem

So, on behalf of tomorrow's teenagers, how can we address the powerful underlying messages of nihilism, naturalism, determinism and moral relativism in Western culture?

First we must recognise that each of these is founded upon an underlying cultural rejection of God. If there is no God then there is no basis for meaning, for anything beyond the natural world, nor for any purposeful action beyond determinism, nor for any moral absolutes. However, if God does exist, then the picture changes radically.

Second, we must recognise that ideas and information all carry with them a deeper message. Whatever is taught explicitly in schools, in homes, or in the media carries with it certain beliefs and values. Notions about who we are which are taught in biology and psychology, for instance, bring with them a set of consequent beliefs about our value and freedom. Ideas about the right to rule, which are taught in history, bring with them a set of consequent beliefs and values about the nature of authority.

If we are concerned about the teenagers of tomorrow, we must make sure that what is taught is true and that the implicit beliefs and values that are carried with it are brought into the open. Let's look at this in relation to schools (but recognising that the need for consistency that we will discover is just as relevant in the home and in the media).

If it truly is the case that God does not exist, that we are simply a set of chemicals and neurones that has evolved by chance, that our behaviour is determined by our genes and our environment, and that there is no ultimate authority – then we must learn to live with the implica-tions of this. That means that we should help our schools to teach this consistently throughout the curriculum. We may find that we have to rewrite most of the current school mission statements. How can a school declare that its pupils must value individuals for who they are, take responsibility for their actions, and have respect for authority – if these beliefs are fundamentally without foundation?

On the other hand, if God does exist, and we are created in his image, with intrinsic value, worth, freedom and authority – then, again, we must learn to live with the implications of this. The school mission statement would be perfectly valid, but we would need to think carefully about the implicit beliefs and values communicated by the curriculum subjects as they are currently taught.

The problem is that in many schools young people are given two conflicting messages. The school mission statement may tell them that everyone is valuable, that everyone should exercise self-control and respect authority. But in biology they may learn that we have evolved through death of the least fit; in psychology they may learn that our behaviour is determined by our genes and environment; in history they may learn that authority is tyranny that should be rejected.

So where do we go from here? If we recognise that we do need to be consistent one way or the other, which way should we go? How can we decide? Clearly, we are driven to that fundamental question: does God exist? It seems that belief in God cannot be simply an issue for individuals. There are many beliefs that individuals hold that are personal and private. Whether or not I believe that Southampton Football Club is a great team to support is really just a private belief for me on my own. However, God's existence is a public rather than a private issue – for it has so many implications for the whole of our culture.

Nietzsche, whom we have met several times in this book, severely criticised people who rejected God but held on to traditional beliefs and values that derive from God. This is one of the few points on which I agree with him. If God does not exist, let's be consistent and, as a culture, not try to hold on to past beliefs and values that stem from him. However, if we look at the lives of many of today's teenagers and begin to see how devastating it has been to let go of those beliefs and values, does that not motivate us to consider seriously whether, in fact, God may actually exist? If we find that he does exist after all then we will know that those beliefs and values that we so desperately need to rediscover as a culture are actually completely well-founded.

When we look at the behaviour of some teenagers and ask the question, 'Why do they do that?' we find that so many of the most powerful fundamental answers seem to be rooted in the philosophical rejection of God which underlies so many of the changes in Western culture. Therefore, the existence or non-existence of God cannot be just a matter for personal, private belief. It has such massive cultural implications, which we can see ultimately being played out in the lives of today's teenagers, that we must consider the question not just as individuals but also as a culture, as a nation, as a community.

Notes

[1] D. Rushkoff, *Children of Chaos (Surviving the End of the World as We Know It)*, HarperCollins, 1997.
[2] Quoted in *Idea* magazine, September 1993.

If Only:
The Search for Happiness
by Nick Pollard

'If only I were rich and successful. If only I were free to do
whatever I wanted, whenever I wanted. If only I were healthy
and secure. Then I would be happy. Then I would be content.'

We spend our lives searching for fulfilment – but are we looking
in the right places?

This book tells the true-life stories of three people in search of
an answer. Andy wants to be a millionaire and doesn't care how
many people he treads on – until he is faced with his own
mortality. Sharon wants to be free to use her body and the
bodies of others – until she ends up in a brothel. Jacqui thinks
she will be happy when she forms her own stable, secure family
– until personal tradgedy strikes.

In reflecting on their experiences, Nick Pollard comes to some
surprising conclusions.

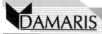
Get More Like Jesus While Watching TV

by Nick Pollard

Get more like Jesus while watching TV
Nick Pollard & Steve Couch

Television – a vital part of modern life, a factor in our moral decline, or simply chewing gum for the eyes?

The effect that television has on us depends as much on what happens in our heads as what happens on-screen. Whether or not we like it (and plenty of us like it a lot) TV is here to stay. But can watching your favourite programmes help you to become more like Jesus?

Get More Like Jesus While Watching TV helps you to look at television in the light of Romans chapter 12, and explores what it means to become more like Jesus in a high-tech, media-saturated world.

DAMARIS